THE CHURCH RENEWED

The Documents of Vatican II Reconsidered

Edited by

George P. Schner

UNIVERSITY
PRESS OF
AMERICA

LANHAM • NEW YORK • LONDON

93763

Copyright © 1986 by

University Press of America,® Inc.

4720 Boston Way
Lanham, MD 20706

3 Henrietta Street
London WC2E 8LU England

Co-published by arrangement with
Regis College, Toronto, Canada

Library of Congress Cataloging in Publication Data

The Church renewed.

Bibliography: p.
1. Vatican Council (2nd : 1962-1965)   2. Catholic
Church—Doctrines.   I. Schner, George P., 1946-
BX830 1962.C49   1986   262'.52   86-13326
ISBN 0-8191-5505-5 (alk. paper)
ISBN 0-8191-5506-3 (pbk. : alk. paper)

IN MEMORY OF
WILLIAM MACBEATH BROWN, C.S.B.

TABLE OF CONTENTS

Foreword

This collection of essays is offered to all who wish to acquaint themselves with the documents of the Second Vatican Council and the scholarship which has reflected upon the Council and its implementation. The common theme of the essays can be stated simply: a careful re-reading of the Council's documents shows that there is still much to be done to accomplish what they set forth as the agenda for renewal.

Not least urgent is the renewal needed to further the ecumenical movement which shaped the documents themselves. This volume is dedicated to MacBeath Brown, a Canadian Basilian priest who gave himself with intense dedication to the work of Christian unity. His life was an inspiration to many, not only for the work of ecumenism and the promotion of social justice, but for the wholehearted living of Gospel values. Though he was already ill in May 1984, when the symposium took place, nevertheless he submitted a paper; it was received with enthusiasm and recognized as a significant contribution to an interpretation of the document on ecumenism.

The members of the symposium were honoured to hear the recollections of another Basilian, George Bernard Cardinal Flahiff, on the first evening of the event. As a historian he introduces the essays of this volume by reminding us of the complex origin of the work of the Council. The remaining essays offer an interpretation of each of the major documents of the Council and some observations about the twenty-five years of implementation which followed.

As editor of this collection I wish to thank the contributors for their labours and acknowledge those who helped prepare the manuscript: Moira Hughes, Ellen Benfaremo, Robert Finlay, S.J., and most especially Maria Horvath for her editorial good sense and patience. I am indebted to the Committee on Intellectual Ministry of the Upper Canadian Province of the Society of Jesus for their encouragement with this project, and to the same Upper Canadian Province for their financial assistance.

Cardinal Flahiff, at the end of the symposium, commented that the essays and the discussion of the assembled participants had taught him much about the documents he had helped to create. I hope your reading of this collection will prove likewise.

George P. Schner
Regis College
25 January 1986

CONTRIBUTORS

Margaret Brennan, I.H.M. — Professor of pastoral theology at Regis College, Toronto, Ontario.

W. MacBeath Brown, C.S.B. — Former assistant director of the Ecumenical Centre in Montreal, Quebec.

Colin Campbell, S.J. — Martin Professor of Political Science, Georgetown University, Washington, D.C.

David Eley, S.J. — Director of the Jesuit Communications Project, Toronto.

Michael Fahey, S.J. — Dean of the Faculty of Theology at St. Michael's College of the University of Toronto.

George Bernard Cardinal Flahiff, C.S.B. — Formerly professor of history at St. Michael's College of the University of Toronto, and Council Father for the Second Vatican Council.

Isidore Gorski — Professor of theology at Campion College, University of Regina, Regina, Saskatchewan.

Attila Mikloshazy, S.J. — Dean of St. Augustine's Seminary, Toronto, Ontario.

Ovey Mohammed, S.J. — Professor of theology at Regis College, Toronto, Ontario.

George Schner, S.J. — Dean and professor of philosophy of religion at Regis College, Toronto, Ontario.

Joseph Schner, S.J. — Dean and professor of psychology at Campion College of the University of Regina, Regina, Saskatchewan.

Carl Starkloff, S.J. — Professor of theology at Regis College, Toronto, Ontario.

INTRODUCTION

Recollections of a Council Father

GEORGE BERNARD CARDINAL FLAHIFF

I would like to begin by saying how delighted I was to receive the invitation from Father Jacques Monet to attend this symposium on the documents of the Vatican II, planned by the Committee on Intellectual Ministry of the Upper Canadian Province of the Society of Jesus. Touching memories were stirred when he added that I was invited chiefly because I had been a Council Father at Vatican II.

Any grave responsibilities that could have been aroused when he further invited me to address you, not just to attend, but to address you at this opening session, were perhaps lightened somewhat when he specified that he was requesting "but a few words of reflection on the experience of the Council." Others, I was told, would be focussing in a much more scholarly way on ten of the major documents of the Council—on their origins, their content, their implementation, and their particular use, especially here in Canada.

Back in 1982, the twentieth anniversary of the opening of the Second Vatican Ecumenical Council on October 11, 1962, a great deal of publicity was given to this anniversary, I think particularly in Catholic periodicals on this continent, in Catholic weekly newspapers, and so on. To cite an example, the *National Catholic Reporter* in the United States published a whole special section of forty long pages on Vatican II exclusively, with hardly even any ads. One may or may not agree with opinions expressed in the *National Catholic Reporter* from week to week, but that particular edition was especially good as an account of Vatican II. It had an abundance of pictures as well as excellent articles from various points of view on Vatican II and its implementation over those twenty years.

To date, your symposium is the only publicity I have seen given to a very important silver jubilee of Vatican II. It was twenty-five years ago,

1

on January 25, 1959, that Pope John XXIII—only three months after his election as Pope—surprised everybody by announcing that he was convoking an Ecumenical Council. Yes, so early in his pontificate, with absolutely no allusion whatsoever before that, to so important a meeting; it did indeed come as a surprise.

Just as surprising, if not more so, was his announcement at Christmas, in 1961, that the Council would begin much earlier than anybody expected, in October of the following year.

One could certainly wonder why John XXIII, already seventy-seven years old when he was elected, would ever think of such an event as an Ecumenical Council. It was only the twenty-first in two thousand years. It must have been what was on his mind, in a very special way, that led him to call the Council. We are told, for instance, that within a month or two of his election, in a somewhat troubled conversation with his Secretary of State about the current condition of the world, and the Church's role in the world at that time, he suddenly cried out, "A council!" The idea came to him at that moment.

He is known, after the Council was announced, to have declared more than once its goal as an "aggiornamento," a bringing up to date, in the sense of meeting the precise and even concrete needs of the time. 'Twas not just the experience of two world wars that made him aware of the situation. The diverse appointments of his career had also contributed a good deal. He had held very few posts in the Vatican, in the Curia there. He did have some minor ones, one for a short time in the central office for the Eastern Churches, then as the Apostolic Visitor (as they called it then, not Apostolic Delegate) to Bulgaria. There, in the very heart of what was then a very troubled Balkan state, he spent ten years. At the end of those ten years, he went on for ten more years to Istanbul, the capital of Turkey. Finally, in 1945, at the age of sixty-three, he was sent to Paris as Papal Nuncio just as the Second World War was coming to an end.

He seems to have fitted extremely well into the situation in Paris, some would say even curiously well. It certainly was not an easy time in the French capital. I did not see it at that time, but the pictures show the destruction in Paris, the upset in the normal Parisian way of life.

While he was in Paris, he was made a cardinal. Then, at the age of seventy-one, in 1952, he became Archbishop or rather, Patriarch of Venice. It was from there that he went to the conclave of 1959, after the death of Pope Pius XII. At this conclave, he was elected to become Pope John XXIII.

All these experiences had made him keenly aware of and sensitive to the concrete needs of the world in that first half and a bit more of the twentieth century. His concern about all these things and about the consequent role of the Church in these situations would certainly have resulted from his personal experiences but even more, I suppose, from his personal sensitivity and from what I am sure was his personal sanctity.

Within the Church itself, he had been aware of breakaways, those that followed Vatican I back in 1870, for instance. He was quite aware of the radical trends that, earlier in the century, had been termed "modernism" and had been condemned by his predecessor, Pope Pius XII. There were many new approaches to the nature and the celebration of the liturgy. These were already well known in Germany and France, and in the middle of this century, they were starting to become important in the United States and also here in Canada. They were enthusiastically welcomed by some, but resisted and even keenly opposed by others.

There were also stresses and strains in the middle of this century even between the Eastern part of our Church and the Roman or Western attitudes. But at that time, relationships with other Christian Churches were important and actually encouraging, especially with the development of what became the World Council of Churches.

What hope was there at that time of any union, reunion, of the various Christian Churches? Pope John XXIII had had personal experience of practically all of these things. As a result, he felt the need of a true updating in the Church and in the Church's relating more fully to the time and to the needs of the time. What "aggiornamento" truly meant for Pope John is clearly and even touchingly expressed in the papal bull he issued on December 25, 1961, to convoke officially the Second Vatican Council for the following year.

Let me read just a few sentences from that document. After a few words of introduction, he goes on:

> Today the Church is witnessing a crisis underway within society. While humanity is on the edge of a new era, tasks of immense gravity and amplitude await the Church, as in the most tragic periods of its history. It is a question in fact of bringing the modern world into contact with the vivifying and perennial energies of the gospel, a world which exults itself with its conquests in the technical and scientific fields, but which brings also the consequences of a temporal order which some have wished to reorganize excluding God. This is why modern society is earmarked by a great material progress to which there is not a corresponding advance in the moral field.
>
> Hence there is a weakening in the aspiration toward the values of the spirit. Hence an urge to the almost exclusive search for earthly pleasures, which progressive technology places with such ease within the reach of all. And hence there is a completely new and disconcerting fact: the existence of a militant atheism which is active on a world level.
>
> These painful considerations are a reminder of the duty to be vigilant and to keep the sense of responsiblity awake. Distrustful souls see only

3

darkness burdening the face of the earth. We, instead, like to reaffirm all our confidence in our Saviour, who has not left the world which He redeemed.

He goes on in the rest of that document to say something about the precise approaches in the Council to deal with such situations.

By the time Pope John issued this official convocation for the Second Vatican Council, my personal interest in it, I would like to note, had become more than a mere curiosity about what might happen. I had been appointed Archbishop of Winnipeg on March 15—yes, the Ides of March—the year 1961. I must admit that one of the things to which I was most sensitive at the news of my appointment was the realization that, in a year and a half, I would be attending the twenty-first Ecumenical Council of the Church, the first one in almost a hundred years.

It was already being prepared by others in Rome. It was a relatively small preparatory commission, as it was called, that had been set up at a very early date to prepare what might be discussed at the Council. At the same time, bishops throughout the world were all invited to express their opinions on questions the Council should consider. In this way, it got a universal response, particularly when two thousand bishops through the world were heard from. Theological universities from all over were also asked to express their opinions.

Documents, which were based largely on these letters and worked out by some five hundred theologians from all parts of the world invited to Rome for study purposes, came to be assigned by the preparatory commission and by other specialized commissions. They were to provide material for discussions in the Council once it opened. The main topics in the Council itself were then handled by commissions set up in the very first days after the Council opened. Each commission dealt with a particular issue, as do our papers in the other sessions here.

There were ten commissions in all at the beginning of the Council, each one made up of twenty-five members—a president, chosen by the Holy Father, sixteen elected in a democratic vote by the members of the Council as a whole, then finally eight more appointed personally by the Holy Father. To each separate commission were further attached consultors chosen from men with special competence and again, the outstanding theologians at that moment in our Church.

One died very recently—Karl Rahner. He was outstanding in the whole Council, but there were many others as well. Some had been under suspicion for some time, but they really came forth for the good of all of us and their work in the Council.

The ten commissions that were set up dealt with the faith and moral issues—some with Scripture, others with bishops, one each with the Oriental Churches, the discipline of the sacraments, the discipline of the

Church and the Christian people, the religious, the missions, the sacred liturgy, seminaries, studies, the Catholic schools, and the apostolate of the laity.

From your knowledge of the four constitutions, nine decrees and three declarations that are the official documents of Vatican II, you would be aware that they were developed under these commissions before ultimately receiving, by general vote in the plenary sessions, the required majority approval of the Council members as a whole. The preparatory work was very interesting, as a matter of fact. Theologians took their place on the commissions. If you were on one of the commissions, you would hear much discussion. I really think there was a great richness to the way the problems were proposed and then discussed and finally brought to a draft at last for voting. Frequently, the draft had to be voted and revoted. I think the one on the Church and the modern world, *Gaudium et Spes*, took up more time than any other two or three.

The normal procedure was to have the commission's original draft of the text presented to each member of the Council for a study. Then the text, as it existed, was debated in general sessions. As the debates proceeded, it was the role of the particular commission of twenty-five to work on all the criticisms, all the proposed amendments, and gradually, as soon as possible, to arrive at a text that ultimately met with the strong majority that was required.

It was only at the end of the four years of the Council that the official texts were finally published. They are, of course, still available in print. I shall not go into detail to precisely how these lengthy discussions, debates, and even controversies went on. They were very profound. This was clearly the case concerning the one on the Church and the modern world. They looked at what should be discussed, how it should be discussed, and what were the goals. They made a revision of sections of it, then revisions of the whole text. (One of the men who made, as I recall, outstanding contributions on that text was a man who, at that time, was a certain Cardinal Wojtyla, now Pope John Paul II.)

Some allusions to differences of opinion may come out in the various papers of our symposium here that deals with these documents and with their influence over the past twenty years. I would like to note a few facts about the composition and the conduct of Vatican II that impressed, intrigued, often surprised me as well as many others. Take, for instance, the number present at Vatican II. Vatican I, in 1869 and 1870, for a part at least had barely five hundred bishops. They all fitted into one transcept of St. Peter's Basilica. We began Vatican II on October 11, 1962, with exactly 2,540 bishops, not counting the theologians or other observers who were there. At least 350 more were eligible but for health or other reasons did not come to that opening session. I do believe though, there was one session—it was a festive occasion—when almost 2,900 bishops were present. It was a truly impressive sight to look up and down the length of St. Peter's and to see them all. It looked like two long bleachers that faced each other along the full length of the nave of St. Peter's. Bishops were clothed in their purple choir dress; the shades of purple from all parts of the world varied greatly. And the variety of the colour of skin on the faces witnessed even more strikingly to the universal character of the Council. Archbishop Pocock, former archbishop here in Toronto, sat next to a very young bishop from a former French colony in Africa. His name was Gautin. He is now a cardinal. In the recent appointments in Rome about two months ago, he was named to succeed Cardinal Baggio in what is one of the greatest of the congregations in Rome.

Each bishop could bring a theologian with him to the Council for his own assistance, particularly in preparing his interventions. All theologians, not only those brought by bishops but those invited by the Council as a whole, or rather, by the commissions as a whole, could attend the plenary sessions; there they offered advice but did not take part in the discussions. However, they did take part fully in the discussions that preceded the final state of these papers. They were always invited to the informal sessions of the ten commissions I mentioned; it is there that they played an important role in reshaping the texts before they were formally adopted in a general session of the Council.

Other attendants were also present, particularly as guests termed "observers." It was Pope John XXIII's idea to invite them in the few weeks before anything formal was done, so that other Churches should be there to observe, to listen, even to help with comments. The number and the variety of these non-Catholics present as observers increased throughout the four years of the Second Vatican Council.

Religious orders and congregations were also represented. For the first two sessions, only male religious were present, but by the third session, we had learned something and there were at least two superiors general of women's congregations, Sister Mary Lou Tobin, from the United States, and the superior general of the Daughters of Charity of St. Vincent de Paul from Paris. By the fourth session, there were at least fifteen to twenty superiors general of women's groups present.

A limited number of laymen were also invited. As I think back over it, most striking among those guests and observers was the number of observer delegates from Churches other than the Roman Catholic Church. Pope John XXIII had planned and arranged this even before the first session in 1962. The World Council of Churches had been invited to send delegates, and it did so. In addition, ten separate Christian denominations were also present; their number increased in the later sessions. There was no formal exchange in the sessions themselves, but there was a great deal of contact outside the sessions, to discuss the

6

reactions of these observer friends or perhaps their suggestions to us of improvements that could be made. The experience of those months, those years even, I think, witnessed to a growing ecumenism of which we have been conscious since the end of the nineteenth century. But it went much further at Vatican II. Informal friendships and exchanges developed.

(Without knowing that he would be here this evening, I had written in my paper that we Canadian bishops saw a great deal of a theologian named Canon Eugene Fairweather. I would like to pay tribute to him tonight for what he contributed to us, if it is not out of line. We would often have, on a Sunday morning—no sessions on Sunday—a grouping of our Canadian bishops. It was there that we benefitted so much from Eugene Fairweather's contributions.)

Gradually, the non-Catholic observers started holding a late afternoon session once a week. They would come together to discuss what they had heard in the general session of Vatican II. Finally, they invited the members of the Ecumenical Council itself to their discussions so they could learn from us and we could learn from them.

In my remarks I have tried not only to present aspects of the historical setting, the structures, and the working of the Council, but also to include my personal experience.

Unlike earlier ecumenical councils, the implementation of the Council, at least as foreseen by Pope John XXIII, was to have nothing to do with putting infallible decrees into effect. Rather, it was concerned with qualifying both the experience and the teaching of Vatican II and with implementing them in the life of the Church, and, please God, to some extent in human life as a whole in our own time and in time to come. Not that this would be at all easy. A keen and varied interest had been evident throughout the whole of Vatican II. The debate of the Council required a personal response. On the whole, the response to that invitation was considerable and stimulating.

Still, there were sharp differences of opinion, sharp differences of conviction. A very considerable majority was required for the votes that approved the official documents of the Council, but negative votes were not minimal at all. We were conscious of some rather radical points of view or, should I say, just forward looking points of view. But we were even more conscious, I think, of reactionary points of view. The convictions of Archibishop Lefèvre, for instance, were very evident in the course of the Council, particularly in its last two sessions. He and a group that shared his views for the most part offered quite active pressures—no violence—but they certainly spoke with conviction. They gathered together regularly to discuss matters and even to prepare introductions. They represented various parts of the world and they came to be known informally in the Council as the Coetus Internationalis. Among the results of Vatican II one would certainly have to list Archbishop Lefèvre's separation, the founding of his Pius X seminary in Switzerland, and the spread of his spirit and his outlook to other parts of the world, perhaps especially in the United States but right here in Canada as well. This is a very striking divergence, but there have been others of a less informal sort.

I suppose one could ask, as I prepare to finish, just what did happen to the spirit of Vatican II as a whole? Did it fail? I certainly do not think so. I think the spirit is still active here. There has been much approval of what happened in the matter of spirit of Vatican II. This is as a result of important developments in many aspects of the Church's way of life. The role of the laity is certainly noticeable. We are also beginning to realize a bit more the role women should play in the Church. Yet there have also been rejections, alterations and the like, not to mention even quite undesirable teachings and actions since the Council ended.

The edition of the *National Catholic Reporter* to which I referred at the beginning of my talk, even if it is not a truly scholarly publication, has articles dealing with resentment, failures, disruptions and the like in the Church since Vatican II. But, it has an even larger number of articles on the continuing success of Vatican II and on the advances that it has produced. I suppose we are all conscious of the pros and the cons in judgments about Vatican II. In an article in *Commonweal* in 1982, Rosemary Haughton is quoted as referring to Vatican II as "that superbly destructive Council." You would have to talk with her to see what she meant by "destructive." An Irish priest, Terrence O'Brien, says in a very recent book, "The great renewal hoped for after Vatican II did not take place." An editorial in our own local *New Catholic Times*, on March 25, 1984, refers to "groups in the Church who have experienced the agony and others who have experienced the ecstasy of Vatican II."

Some have mused over a possible question: Should Vatican II have continued longer in the hope of arriving at a unanimous reaction in implementing principles? It would not have been easy to do. There was, I think, a majority opinion that much had truly been accomplished and prolonging discussions yet further would only have increased the tensions that even then certainly existed. I do not think we would have wanted to repeat the Council of Trent and its eighteen years. I doubt if any ecumenical council, even back to the first one in Nicaea in 325, has ever been completely free of subsequent dissatisfaction or even dissent. As a result of the documents of Vatican II, and our study, our exchanges and so on, the question for us here at this symposium is simply, *Quid faciendum*?

But how will we know the context in which we are asking this question? The media, for instance, and the diversity of presentations and judgments make it difficult for us to provide answers, especially if we are now aware of the conflicting interpretations or consciously seeking the truth. If we are to answer the question, we must see ourselves as members of the Church, of God's family, of the Mystical Body of Christ. In seeing ourselves in that role, we must ask, *Quid faciendum*?

Perhaps conditions in this last quarter of the twentieth century prevent a simple answer to this question, but the Church certainly has a role to play as in that passage I quoted to you from John XXIII. It is not on the spiritual aspect alone; it is the effect on the material, on the purely human, all those other aspects of our life here.

A symposium, like the present one, basically not dealing with the Council's agony or for that matter with its ecstasy, but dealing with conclusions arrived at can look at answers to that *Quid faciendum*. Always under the guidance of the Holy Spirit, of course, such a symposium can be extremely useful and, please God, truly fruitful. So, I think I should close with a prayer—*Veni Sancte Spiritus*.

COMMENTARY ON THE

Dogmatic Constitution on the Church

Lumen Gentium

MICHAEL FAHEY

One of the delightful occasional rituals within a family circle is to take down from the shelf the dusty photo albums to share, especially with the younger generation, the chronicle of how the family has changed. While poring over the photos, the young recognize resemblances, they see continuity of family traditions, and they understand what changes have occurred. In the Roman Catholic Church, as Vatican II becomes more and more an event of a previous generation, all of us, young and old, family members and friends, need to look at the way we were then to understand who we are now and what we want to become.

Now that the Catholic Church has celebrated the twentieth anniversary of Vatican II's *Dogmatic Constitution on the Church, Lumen Gentium* (November 21, 1964), it is useful to reflect back over these years.[1] Twenty years is only a modest anniversary, whether it be for an individual's birthday or for a business merger; it is all the more modest in the life of a two-thousand-year-old church. How have this text and other Vatican II documents stood up? Do they still meet the important questions in the 1980's?

A number of far-reaching changes have occurred in those twenty years. Relations with non-Catholics have undergone profound shifts: conversations are underway between Catholics and other Christians, like the Orthodox, Anglicans and Lutherans; and Roman Catholic theologians have now been officially appointed by the Vatican to participate in the Faith and Order Commission of the World Council of Churches, the section responsible for preparing theological position papers such as the Lima document *Baptism, Eucharist and Ministry* of 1982. Dramatic changes have also occurred for Catholics in the way that Sunday mass, the Eucharist, is celebrated in parishes—the use of the vernacular, the altar facing the people, more participation by the

11

faithful, and women in the sanctuary to read the Scripture lessons and to serve as auxiliary ministers of the Eucharist. Through episcopal conferences, bishops speak out on public issues related to the economy, nuclear disarmament and medical procedures.

To focus on the text of *Lumen Gentium* in isolation from other Council texts would create a lopsided picture of how the Council envisaged the Church. In order to appreciate the vision of Church in Vatican II, it is necessary to draw upon other statements about Church life interspersed in additional texts on the inner workings of the Church, its role in the modern world, the vocation of all the baptized, the responsibilities of bishops and priests, the relationship of the Catholic Church with other Christian Churches, and religious freedom. What is needed is a synthesis of all the texts of Vatican II rather than a minute analysis of each and every paragraph. The work of unifying into a splendid whole still remains an unfinished task.

A small committee, the Theological Preparatory Commission, had drafted a working document on the Church for the Council's first session. This working paper's vision of the Church showed little progress over the ecclesiology that had been traditional in the theological manuals used in many Catholic seminaries since the close of Vatican I in 1870. When the commission's chairman, Cardinal Ottaviani, introduced this preparatory schema in December 1962, some seventy-eight bishops spoke during the next six days—almost all urged a major revision of the text. Cardinal Suenens of Brussels recommended the formation of a new commission to prepare two documents, one a reworked text on the Church's inner structure and another on the Church's tasks in the world to promote justice, peace and cultural development. The first document is now known as *Lumen Gentium*; the second document, first known simply as *Schema 13*, eventually became the *Pastoral Constitution on the Church in the Modern World, Gaudium et Spes*. Here, for the first time, a Council touched on "earthly realities" such as work, political life and scientific achievements.

The contribution of Vatican II to the life of the Roman Catholic Church was not simply the promulgation of various texts. The Council enriched the understanding of not only the more than two thousand bishops and their advisers during the four sessions from 1962 to 1965 but also of those who followed the Council's proceedings through press or popular books. Such collective experiences help us to interpret the published documents that otherwise would seem to be merely words.

Those who attended the Council celebrated catholicity, that universality that has always been a mark of the Church. The catholicism that they experienced at the Council was one far more culturally and theologically diverse than they had previously imagined. Those national hierarchies that were timid came to express a new freedom, even to disagree on the pastoral tasks of the Church.

During the initial days of the first session, the bishops recognized their responsibility to do more than to rubber stamp texts written in advance. Insights grew and the texts changed as bishops realized that the Council's success depended on them, that even with the Holy Spirit's assistance, the Council could fail if its members were deaf to the Spirit's promptings.

The bishops learned much as they came together daily as a group, listened to numerous interventions and heard lectures from specialists who described practices flourishing in some parts of the Church. The liturgical diversity and the variety of attitudes toward the institutional structures of Catholicism emphasized the fact that the Church was far more complex than a single diocese or nation. This encouraged the bishops to turn to support experiments that had been developing in parishes, universities, monasteries or basic Christian communities, but which had aroused suspicion in the past. They understood that they were not creating something totally new; they were giving approval and encouragement to practices already at work. Unlike Trent and Vatican I, the goal of this Council would not be to codify, catalogue or condemn but to erect guideposts for the future.

The bishops' learning did not end with the closing ceremonies in 1965. Each bishop had to return to his diocese to communicate his vision of the Council. Some bishops seemed more comfortable with change than others. Some were more articulate in explaining the new agenda. Others believed that change threatened the Church's continuity with the past and thought the faithful needed to be protected.

Of all the documents that emerged from Vatican II, major attention has been given to *Lumen Gentium*. This is a truly remarkable document that overcomes the legalism, triumphalism and clericalism of so many earlier official texts on the Church. Unlike the rejected earlier draft that began with a self-confident defence of the Church militant, the final text begins with a description of the mystery of the Blessed Trinity's love for humanity expressed in the formation of a new People of God in Christ.

The final text on the Church differs from many Roman documents published between 1870 and 1960 that were legalistic and condemnatory. Its opening sections are marked with a strong biblical flavour and most chapters are pastorally sensitive. The constitution stresses the mystery dimension of the Church, which is described neither as an institution nor a "perfect society" with charter, rules and infra-structures. It is rather a pilgrim people, a sojourning Church moving toward fulfilment in the future. The word "Church" designates those commissioned with special responsibility and the totality of believers graced with the

Holy Spirit's charisms. (The earlier version of *Lumen Gentium* had placed statements about the hierarchy before any treatment of the People of God as a whole.)

In *Lumen Gentium*, the bishops struggled to find a formula to indicate who were members of the Church, who belonged to the Church of Christ. At the Council, the Church was not described as simply coextensive with the Roman Catholic Church as had been stated in Pius XII's encyclical *Mystici Corporis Christi* in 1943. Eventually, the Council came up with a more subtle formulation. Instead of saying that the Church of Christ *is* the Roman Catholic Church, the text states that the Church of Christ *subsists in* the Roman Catholic Church, thereby admitting that it is also alive in other Churches and communities not in full communion with Catholicism (8). Other convictions about "sister Churches" were described in the *Decree on Ecumenism*, especially article 3: "all those justified by faith through baptism are incorporated into Christ." These Christians are fellow believers even if they are not in full communion with the Church of Rome. Thus, the term "Church" (or ecclesial community) can describe other Christian groups.

Such ecumenical sensitivity may seem very obvious today, but in view of Catholic hostility to Protestant unity efforts in the first half of this century, the shift among Catholics is startling.

Despite the importance of Vatican II's documents, only a small number of people inside and outside the Catholic Church—a few religious educators, scholars, seminarians and priests—have read or studied them. Often they are only familiar with a few passages not even central to the major thrust of the Council.

This not surprising because, even with two acceptable English versions, the constitutions and decrees of the Council are difficult to read. They require a technical, clerical training that few persons possess or want to possess. Certain terms popularized in Vatican II have come into usage among Catholics: People of God, charisms, collegiality, signs of the times, ecumenism, hierarchy of truths. But the texts themselves have minimal appeal, unlike the four gospels, whose teachings are easily understood by people from many cultures and eras. Even the recent statements by the Anglican/Roman Catholic International Commission affirming consensus on topics such as baptism, Eucharist, ministry and authority, or the documents on papal primacy produced by the Lutheran/Roman Catholic dialogue in the United States are easier to read than the texts of Vatican II.

This general lack of familiarity with the Council texts raises a problem about the reception of Vatican II. By "reception" theologians refer to a process of acceptance of specific Council or other Church teachings.[2] In this way, the Church at large comes to judge whether formulations and emphases of various Church leaders on different teachings are sufficiently comprehensive. Reception is a progressive recognition by Christians that some official texts are more appropriate and more lasting as authentic expressions of Christian belief than other statements. Reception is made possible by a gift or sixth sense bestowed upon the faithful as a whole, a *sensus fidelium* (believers' instinct).

How will reception of the texts of Vatican II take place if they are poorly known? It is not by approving formulas. Reception will be more in the nature of personal assimilation of attitudes, actions, conversions, all fostered by the life of the Church and given expression in the Council texts.

Those who have studied the Vatican II texts have identified an internal order of importance, the "hierarchy of truths" (UR 11), whereby a specific degree of importance is assigned to a Christian doctrine. Hence, for example, belief in the Trinity is more important than belief in purgatory. But there exists also a "hierarchy of expression." Eventually the Church at large will be able to measure the relative degree of success the Council had in all efforts to express its convictions. Some of these expressions will be more felicitous than others. Catholic theologians like Yves Congar have also spoken of a "hierarchy of councils." By this he assigns greater importance to some specific Councils than to others. For instance, he would assign greater importance to those Councils of the first millenium when the Churches of the East and West were one and undivided than the General Councils of the West, including the Councils of Trent and Vatican I, that spoke merely for the Catholic Church of the West.

Why are some passages in texts of Vatican II unsatisfactory? The reasons vary. Often one reason was a lack of time or theological expertise to grapple with a difficult question. Another was the composition of a drafting committee. Because Vatican I, the previous Council, had taken place so many years ago, no one at this Council had any experience of how best to proceed. Even at the election of a new pope in a conclave of 110 cardinals, procedures can be complex and complicated; they were all the more complicated at Vatican II where more than two thousand persons had the right to speak and vote.

Even though no one has suggested that the texts of Vatican II are as inspired or inerrant as the books of the Bible, some of the early commentaries were so rhapsodic about the documents that they took on the aura of finished pieces of work. Furthermore, the theologians who had a hand in the composition of the texts would naturally be slow to criticize the finished product. At first, the critical comments came from the Orthodox and Protestant observers. But now, in retrospect, Catholics are prepared to note, in the Council texts, various ambiguities, unanswered questions, problematic older formulations and the absence of originality in handling such questions as the authority of the pope or what elements in the Church are of divine origin (*jus divinum*), the status of ordained ministers in other Churches and the possibility of intercommunion among Christians.

Some texts are disappointing because of their lack of clarity and a patronizing tone toward the laity, who were not present to express their own views. Forged in a mixture of modern languages, translated into Latin before the final voting took place, retranslated into modern languages again for distribution throughout the local Churches, the texts lack literary elegance. Some texts are serenely ambiguous so as not to offend specific minority opinions. Finally, one cannot eliminate the possibility that certain formulations are unsatisfactory because the Council Fathers, or at least their more vocal spokesmen, lacked the courage and imagination to reformulate teachings that might have had important ramifications on life in the Church today.

How can the Council's message and spirit be kept alive among the millions of Christians who are unlikely to read or study the texts year after year? Especially for the specialist, the texts will remain important as milestones. But for most, the message of the Council will be preserved and communicated more by symbolic gestures, actions and events, some seen on television or in photographs. For instance, the effort to eliminate certain monarchical trappings from the papal office led to a reformulation of language about the papacy at Vatican II. But most people learned about this when the papal tiara was replaced by the simple bishop's pallium, rather than by any words stating that the pope is not a monarch but a servant. Collegiality is described in several sections of *Lumen Gentium*, but the sight of a national hierarchy speaking out on a social or economic issue more effectively expresses that teaching. Co-responsibility of the ordained and of the non-ordained alike in building up the Church is also described here, but that teaching is best communicated through well-run parish councils, national workshops and the sharing of roles in the liturgy. Principles for ecumenism are explained in the texts of Vatican II, but what will be remembered are gestures of reconciliation and love, like the embrace between Pope Paul VI and Eastern Orthodox Patriarch Athenagoras on Jerusalem's Mount of Olives in 1964, or Pope Paul's falling onto his knees to kiss the feet of Orthodox Metropolitan Meliton while they prayed together in the Sistine Chapel in 1975. And Pope John Paul I's kneeling and praying at the side of Orthodox Metropolitan Nikodim of Leningrad, who suffered a fatal heart attack during an audience with that pope in 1978, shows more than any words can that the Churches of the East and West are sister Churches.

The texts of Vatican II will retain their importance especially for the expert, but the spirit of the Council will be shared among most people by visible gestures. Nonetheless, it would be useful to explain those

16

symbolic actions in some kind of simplified paraphrasing of the Council documents. No disrespect is intended if it is stated that some of the Council texts were written in haste and need to be reformulated and that some translations need to be redone to remove noninclusive, sexist language. Many can participate in this joint effort. Such work is similar to regular updating by the International Commission of English in the Liturgy, which improves translations of rituals, especially the Eucharistic prayers.

The truth of Christianity is not found in grammar or stylistics or even in theological niceties. Carefully articulated texts are only one form. The Council will not have achieved its goal merely if the texts become more polished. Closer to the heart of the Council are gestures of reconciliation symbolizing interior conversion and an ever-greater openness to God's presence. Therefore, the greatest compliment one could pay to *Lumen Gentium* would be not to go over it line by line, analyzing and drawing subtle distinctions, but to build on this text and to put the teaching into action. The goal of familiarity with the Vatican decrees is not to freeze them but to appreciate what they are saying about the Church's need to be conformed to Gospel values.

Directors of religious education in local churches and dioceses are sometimes challenged by demands for a return to the basics, to the fundamentals, to the clear teachings and perhaps even to a question-and-answer catechism suitable for memorization. Still, it needs repeating that even the Church's best expressions of belief, that is, the creeds, prayers, rituals, are quite lifeless if what is spoken and prayed is not practised.

Since *Lumen Gentium* was promulgated in 1964, much has changed in the Roman Catholic Church: new ways of celebrating the sacraments, new attitudes toward the other Christian Churches, developments about collegiality of bishops, new Church involvement in social justice, broader tolerance for diversity and pluralism in Church life and theology, a new vocabulary to help the Church rethink what may have been entrenched, and new emphases on ways of inculturating the Christian faith in nations that are not European nor North American. Despite some suspicions and fears, the Catholic Church has by and large remained peaceful amid these changes. But there are signs of confrontation between Church officials and certain theologians or groups of persons.

Strictly speaking, Vatican II was not a completely creative event but rather a confirmation of much of what had gone before, an acceptance of aspects of Church life that were in danger of being forgotten, an acceptance of attitudes that were initially frowned upon. At Vatican II, the Catholic Church reaffirmed and encouraged much that was alive and healthy but which had not been stressed in Vatican directives or even papal encyclicals. Nevertheless, Vatican II was largely a reflection on

Church life in the 1940's and 1950's. It is not surprising then that the Council does not address all of the present concerns. There is a certain remoteness in the texts.

If the experience of the Catholic Church in the last forty years can teach us a lesson today, it is the possibility that within the Church now are certain elements neglected by many unofficial teachings that are feared and considered suspect, ideas that are alive but only in small pockets of the world, which can be, indeed will be, blessed by the Church in the future. What might be some of those elements of Church life? Issues that could perhaps affect Catholicism in the twenty-first century include convictions about the need for basic Christian communities, liberation theology, newer forms of ministry with wider responsibility for women and re-articulations of some traditional dogmas. Because it was describing a pilgrim Church, a sojourning Church, Vatican II invites us to be open to the future as we reflect on the experiences of the past.

Notes

1.   There are many commentaries on *Lumen Gentium*, most of which appeared shortly after the text's publication. Among the best are J. Miller, ed., *Vatican II: An Interfaith Appraisal* (Notre Dame: University of Notre Dame Press, 1966); G. Barauna, ed., *L'Eglise de Vatican II: Etudes autour de las Constitution sur L'Eglise*, 2 vols. (Paris: Cerf, 1967); and B. Kloppenburg, *The Ecclesiology of Vatican II* (Chicago: Franciscan Herald Press, 1974). More recent works include Yves Congar, *Le Concile de Vatican II: Son Eglise, Peuple de Dieu et Corps du Christ* (Paris: Beauchesne, 1984); and Karl Rahner, "Concern for the Church," *Theological Investigations*, 20 (New York: Crossroad, 1981), especially chaps. 6 and 7. Among non-Catholic reactions to the document are Bernard C. Pawley, ed., *The Second Vatican Council: Studies by Eight Anglican Observers* (London: Oxford University Press, 1967); and G.C. Berkouwer, *The Second Vatican Council and the New Catholicism* (Grand Rapids: Eerdmans, 1965).
2.   See Edward J. Kilmartin, "Reception in History: An Ecclesiological Phenomenon and Its Significance," *Journal of Ecumenical Studies*, 21 (1984), 34–54.

COMMENTARY ON THE

Pastoral Constitution on the Church in the Modern World

Gaudium et Spes

MICHAEL STOGRE

Schema 13, the *Pastoral Constitution on the Church in the Modern World*, better known as *Gaudium et Spes*, is the best known and most controversial document of Vatican II.[1] It has become the symbol for embodying major shifts in Church thinking.

For some critics of the Church, like Paul Blanchard, these shifts are hardly earth-shattering, and can be called a success only if measured against the Roman Catholic Church's own history:

> In terms of the movement of western culture, however, the council moved so slowly that it almost stood still. In an age when culture and science had moved further in two centuries than the whole world had progressed up to that point in time, Vatican II chose to cling to dogmas and policies that were centuries out of date, dogmas and policies that could be abandoned without any surrender of spiritual ideals. In terms of the 20th century velocity, the council brought Catholicism from the 13th to the 17th century, no mean achievement, but it still left this largest segment of world Christianity 300 years behind the times.[2]

Blanchard's remarks wonderfully concentrate the mind as we approach the documents once more, twenty years later. But he is wrong about *Gaudium et Spes*; I agree with John O'Malley[3] that Vatican II was a reformation in its own right. Furthermore, this document initiated a transformation in the Church that has been far-reaching in only twenty years of pastoral praxis.

At the same time, I concur with Karl Rahner in his seminal article "Towards a Fundamental Theological Interpretation of Vatican II" that the real work has only just begun. The Church in *Gaudium et Spes*, Rahner says, becomes "conscious of its responsibility for the dawning history of humanity. It was truly a Council of the World Church."[4]

Just as Luke and the Acts are now seen as a unity—one work in two volumes—so is *Gaudium et Spes* seen as the compliment of *Lumen Gentium*. The very title of the latter (Light of Nations) invites an application to the vast field of human history and the pastoral needs of the modern world. Therefore, after examining the nature of the Church in *Lumen Gentium*, the Council turned to chart the mission of the Church in the world today.[5]

Like the separate decrees on mission and relations with other religious bodies, the aim of this document is also evangelical: "The Church believes that the key, the center, and the purpose of the whole of human history is to be found in its Lord and Master" (10). The Church wants to enter into "dialogue" with humankind (3) and by reading "signs of the times" (4), to find new ways of sharing its riches with the whole human family (2).

The preface sets the tone. It introduces a theme that will loom large in post-conciliar developments, especially the "preferential option for the poor." The very first line of the document points in that direction:

> The joy and hope, the grief and anguish of the men of our time, especially of those who are poor or afflicted in any way, are the joy and hope, the grief and anguish of the followers of Christ (1).

Another dominant theme in the preface is solidarity. This flows from a renewed theology of the Church which sees itself first of all as the pilgrim "People of God" rather than as a hierarchical body or "perfect society" (*societas perfecta*). In this perspective, the Church desires to accompany the human family on its pilgrimage through history; at the same time, it offers a spirit of co-operation in the efforts to establish a new world order.

In the introduction, the Council Fathers try to read the signs of the time and to outline the central questions facing humanity. They see the world undergoing massive cultural change. This is summed up in their realization that the "destiny of the human race is viewed as a complete whole, no longer, as it were, in the particular histories of various peoples: now it emerges into a complete whole" (5).

The rapidity of cultural and technological change has produced a spiritual malaise: "small wonder then that many of our contemporaries are prevented by this complex situation from recognizing permanent values and duly applying them to recent discoveries" (4).

The structures of traditional societies that have shaped and guided human life are now breaking down. But there is a hint of new freedom within this ferment: "peoples...especially where ancient traditions are still strong, are at the same time conscious of the need to exercise their freedom in a more mature and personal way" (6).

These changes and this new freedom are a challenge to the religions of the world. Increasingly, people are giving up their religious practice, while others are finding, in their search for meaning, a renewed faith commitment.

The political divisions and economic disparities in the world which the Council faced twenty years ago are still present—and more evident to all. The huge debt crises of so many developing nations have brought the problems to a head in the 1980's.

There is also a heightened concern to frame a new world order, to "set up a worldwide community" in which we have "the duty and ability to strengthen our mastery over nature and of the need to establish a political, social, and economical order at the service of humanity" (9).

In the various agencies of the United Nations and in many of the existing international organizations, the Church sees the first attempts at laying the foundation for a new international community (84). This does not suggest one monolithic nation state or the dominance of one or other super-power, but a community of communities where certain functions, like the regulation of international trade or the development of ocean resources, would be determined by a new transnational level of government with real authority to ensure the common good of all peoples.

The introduction ends with a subtle reference to Colossians in which Christ is the "image of the invisible God, the firstborn of all creation" (Col 1:15). This Pauline-inspired letter is highly appropriate because it advocates a mission theology cosmic in scope: the total ministry of the Church is the best means of heralding the Gospel, of being the sacrament of Christ's presence in the world, and of addressing unbelief.[6]

Finally, the introduction outlines the division that will structure the rest of the decree: "to unfold the mystery that is humankind, and to cooperate in tackling the main problems facing the world today" (10).

Part 1: The Church and Humanity's Vocation

Part 1 looks at the mystery of humanity and the human person. In this section, the nature of the human person is developed in a traditional manner. To be human is to be composed of a body with an immortal soul.

This Aristotelian Greek view is somewhat out of step with the biblical view of humanity. The Semitic understanding of the human person is relational in contrast: the body is not just the physical aspect but the whole person as related to and rooted in the material world; the psyche (soul) is not a second component but once again the whole person as possessing interiority and capable of reflection; finally, a third aspect, spirit (pneuma), is also the whole person seen as open to and capable of a relationship with God. More basically, spirit is the principle of life. In summary then, we are animated bodies rather than incarnate spirits.

In any case, the Council Fathers proceeded to ground the dignity of the human person in a two-fold manner. First, they point to a biblical/theological perspective: human beings are made in the image of God. Since this could be understood in an individualistic sense, they are quick to qualify it. They note the partnership of male and female as the fullest expression of this imaging of God. Thus, a communal aspect of personhood is asserted at the outset and further developed in chapter 2 (12). Second, as rational and free, and each with a conscience, human beings can be held accountable for their lives and works.

The Christian anthropology just outlined includes a realization that humanity sinned and was alienated from its creator. This state of sin-separation helps to explain the disorder of the world (13).

It is only in the revelation of Christ, the new human being, that we can fully understand our human dignity and our destiny. This truth gives an urgency to proclaiming the good news of evangelizing the world (15).

These foundational principles are systematically applied in part 2 of the document.

Atheism

Given the theological anthropology just described, it is appropriate that chapter 1 features a discussion of atheism. Humanity, according to the Church, can only find its dignity ultimately in a communion with the Creator. Atheisms, practical or theoretical, that deny this are a grave attack on the dignity of the human person. But despite its clear condemnation of unbelief, this document espouses a compassionate pastoral approach.

Conscience must be respected. Consequently, there may be atheists of good will with whom we may be called to collaborate in building the earth. The document is faithful to an integral vision of evangelization that includes service (diaconia), communion (koinonia) as well as proclamation (kerygma). In their discussion of atheism, the Council Fathers note that a principal cause of unbelief is the way of life of the unbelievers themselves:

> To the extent that they are careless about their instruction in the faith, or present its teachings falsely, or even fail in their religious, moral, or social life, they must be said to conceal rather than to reveal the true nature of God and of religion (19).

This pastoral decree addresses Marxism as one of the principal forms of current atheism. Karl Marx, as is well known, described religion as the "opium of the people." To combat this false view, the Council

Fathers framed what is perhaps their strongest statement:

> One of the gravest errors of our time is the dichotomy between the faith
> which many profess and the practice of their daily lives...Let there, then,
> be no such pernicious opposition between professional and social activity
> on the one hand and religious life on the other. The Christian who shirks
> his temporal duties shirks his duties towards his neighbour, neglects God
> himself, and endangers his eternal salvation (43).

Chapter 2: THE COMMUNITY OF HUMANKIND

Building on, but basically repeating, two social encyclicals of that
period, *Pacem in Terris* (1963) and *Mater et Magistra* (1961), this chapter reiterates Catholic social teaching. Where it does break new ground
is in the invocation of the Trinity as a model for the human community:

> The Lord Jesus Christ when praying to the Father "that they may all be
> one...even as we are one" (Jn 17:21–22) has opened up new horizons
> closed to human reason by implying that there is a certain parallel
> between the union existing among the divine persons and the union of the
> sons of God in truth and love (24).

In addition, it encapsules, in the term "socialization," the growing
reality and realization of the interdependence of all peoples. This is not
to be confused with socialism. Socialization refers to the multiplication
of social relationships so characteristic of the modern age. The complex
tissue of human relationships may well in the end call for new ways of
owning and distributing goods, but this is not discussed at this point.

Of special note in section 27 is the concern to combat "all offenses
against life itself." Here is the seed for the growing consistency of
Church teaching on life issues, from abortion, through capital punish-
ment, to nuclear war itself. It affirms the human rights of all—even of
enemies and those the Church considers in error.

One of these is the right to participate in the production and protection of the common good. This has come to be known as social justice.

The emphasis, then, in this chapter is on Christian social responsibility mandated when Christ established a "communion of his own body,
the Church, in which everyone as members of one another would render
mutual service in the measure of the different gifts bestowed" (32).

This concentration on human rights and the growing reliance on biblical theology instead of philosophy continued in the post-conciliar Church.

Chapter 3: HUMAN ACTIVITY IN THE UNIVERSE

The pastoral constitution affirms human temporal progress as good but
asks: "To what goal is all this individual and collective enterprise
headed?" (33). The universe suffered with humanity the consequences
of sin, yet both are destined to be liberated, to be transformed. How this

will be accomplished remains a mystery. But, since it is basically the Paschal Mystery, some insight is possible.

Having made this link between human history and the Paschal Mystery, the Council Fathers introduce a cautionary note: "We must be careful to distinguish earthly progress clearly from the increase of the Kingdom of Christ; such progress is of vital concern to the Kingdom of God, insofar as it can contribute to the better ordering of human society" (39).

This crucial linkage between progress and the Kingdom remains one of the great unresolved issues of Vatican II. Because the position espoused represents a compromise, further theological reflection is necessary. In fact, the rise of political and liberation theologies in recent decades are attempts to meet this important need.[7]

The central assertion of this section is really the "autonomy of earthly affairs" (36). From this flows the compatibility of faith and science "because the things of the world and the things of faith derive from the same God." Thus, the Church wishes to acknowledge that "the gradual discovery, exploitation, and ordering of the laws and values of matter and society "are perfectly in harmony with the designs of the Creator."

Chapter 4: ROLE OF THE CHURCH IN THE MODERN WORLD

The final chapter of part 1 recapitulates the discussion so far, by applying the principles enunciated to the Church's dialogue with individuals, society, and temporal affairs.

The Church first recognizes its indebtedness to the world: "the Church learned in its early history to express the Christian message in the concepts and languages of different peoples and tried to clarify it in the light of the wisdom of their philosophers" (40).

The Church also admits that structures and methods developed in the secular world can benefit the running of the Church insofar as it is also a visible social structure subject to the same laws and dynamics. The development of modern means of communication now used by the Churches in so many ways would be the most obvious example of this relationship.

Even enemies and persecutors are seen as benefactors (44). This point is not developed; I assume it means that opposition has forced the Church to improve the articulation of its message, as well as to witness to it.

For the individual, the Church proposes a solution to the meaning of existence, reinforces the dignity of the human person, and promotes the rights of humanity (41).

For society, the Church strives to become a model of a universal community that will act as a leaven in overcoming the barriers to a new world order. In this gargantuan effort, the Church promises its co-operation in creating the institutions necessary for the new order and, above all, tries to inspire "commitment, direction, and vigor" (42) in its members to achieve these lofty goals.

With respect to temporal affairs, the Council maintains that it has no "mission in the political, economic or social order" (42). Yet it exhorts its members to imitate Christ "who worked as a craftsman; let them be proud of the opportunity to carry out their earthly activity in such a way as to integrate human, domestic, professional, scientific and technical enterprises with religious values, under whose supreme direction all things are ordered to the glory of God" (43). The two claims seem to reflect different ways of looking at the nature of the Church. The first statement about having no mission in the temporal field reflects the hierarchical view, while the exhortation to involvement is based on a People of God/Servant-Healer perspective. In this latter approach, the laity have a rightful role to play in the world, not just as citizens but as Christians. (This theme is elaborated in the *Decree on the Apostolate of the Laity*, which is discussed elsewhere in this book.)

Finally, the chapter ends with a biblical vision of complete reconciliation in which Christ will "unite all things,...things in heaven and things on earth" (Eph 1:10). This is a fitting conclusion. As Donald Senior points out:

> The missionary theology of Colossians and Ephesians forms therefore one of the most powerful statements in the New Testament concerning the universal missionary nature of the Church. No longer can the Church's horizons be narrow, its agenda timid. It serves a cosmic Lord: therefore its field of service is as wide as the world.[8]

Before turning to future developments and prospects, I will now examine the issues the dogmatic section discusses.

Part 2: Urgent Problems

The preface to the second part singles out six issues: "marriage and the family, culture, economic and social life, politics, the solidarity of peoples, and peace" (46).

There exists a certain parallelism with part 1: it starts over with the person in the basic ecclesial community of family, links this progressively with the social contexts of modern life, and looks towards a new world community that will live in peace, having abolished war and the injustices that lead to it.

It is worth noting that the turn to the historical and the concrete situation is exemplified in each of the chapters of part 2. The topic is always introduced with a description of the problem. The experience of the issue may not be elaborately described but it is included nonetheless.

This methodology foreshadows the major shift in approach that accelerated after the Council and culminated in the apostolic letter *Octogesimo Adveniens*.[9]

The sections on marriage and the family, and on atheism were the two most controversial. For example, the issue of birth control was left to a commission that finally gave rise to *Humanae Vitae*.

It is important to note here one major advance. Marriage was formerly seen as a hierarchy of purposes centred on procreation. In *Schema 13*, this has been overcome by looking at marriage as a covenant of life and love. This text accentuates the mutual love of the spouses as important in itself (49). One flaw, however, is that the teaching seems relevant only in the developed countries where the average family can afford to meet the needs and desires of its members.

Post-conciliar teaching on this subject, which continues in this idealistic vein,[10] is less helpful for the millions of families living under Third World conditions, where their sheer survival is the greatest challenge and over-population is a growing threat. But at least the social teaching of the Church, both within Vatican II and afterwards, has sought to overcome the conditions that make family life so difficult.

Chapter 2: THE DEVELOPMENT OF CULTURE

Culture can be defined as a way of life shaped by meanings and values. Every human being is immersed in culture. We take it for granted, like the atmosphere. This modern dynamic notion of culture differs markedly from the classical approach that held sway in the Church for so long.

The inclusion of culture as a theme and the approach taken form perhaps the most innovative section of the whole document. This was pointed out at a symposium at Notre Dame University in November 1983. There Hervé Carrier described three influences that shaped this section.[11]

The first was the influence of ethnologists and the development of cultural anthropology in this century. As Bernard Lonergan is fond of saying, we have shifted to a pluralistic empirical notion of culture.[12] This understanding is taken up in article 53 of *Gaudium et Spes*: "One can speak about a plurality of cultures. Different styles of living and different scales of values originate in different ways of using things, of working, and self expression, of practicing religion and of behavior..."

Carrier also sees the influence of Marx in the text. He refers in particular to a method of class analysis that defines the dominators of culture and those whose culture is shaped by the dominant elites. This approach to culture, he goes on to say, "contains a dynamic and voluntaristic aspect: the proletarians, dominated by the culture of the bourgeoisie, will have to fight to change their culture."[13]

26

Finally, the political liberation of more than one hundred nations since the Second World War has brought to the fore the quest for cultural rights and identity. For too long, he says, because development models did not sufficiently take culture into consideration, they were often doomed to frustration and failure.[14]

It has also become increasingly apparent to the Church that it must pay close attention to cultural contexts and forms if it wants to proclaim the Good News to "all creation" (Mk 16:15). At the same time, rapid cultural diffusion is homogenizing the different cultures, creating a world-wide culture that would threaten especially the traditional ones. The Church tries to balance the advantages of modern technological culture on the one hand, with the legacy and wisdom of ancient traditions on the other (54, 56).

In brief, then, we must be responsible stewards not just of creation but of cultures as well. Thus, a dynamic rather than static perspective is upheld (55).

The Church really has only two choices about the evangelization of cultures. In recent centuries an "acculturation" approach has been dominant: the evangelist first introduces the culture of the sending nation to the hearer of the word, then preaches the Gospel within this cultural framework. In contrast, the position espoused by the Council is characterized by the term "enculturation." This mode is receptor-oriented that tries to preach the Gospel in the language of, and to express the faith in, the cultural forms of the receiving people.

Neither case can avoid the mediation of culture, for whatever is received is done so according to the mode of the receiver.[15] In theory, the Church has repudiated the former option; it must now develop the skills to actualize the latter.

Chapter 3: ECONOMIC AND SOCIAL LIFE

Faithful to its vision of the dignity of the person, the *Pastoral Constitution on the Church in the Modern World* subordinates all social, economic, and political structures to this principle (63).

As the Church is well aware, this is a most difficult task. The present world structures often do just the opposite. Therefore, the Church, understood as the People of God but especially of the laity, must transform structures so that all people can live in dignity.

In addition to the reiteration of basic social teaching, noteworthy in this section is a return to biblical and patristic thinking. For example, although private property, profit and investment are affirmed as legitimate, they do have a "social mortgage" attached to them. The gifts of creation are meant for the benefit of all human beings. Consequently, it reminds Christians that, in a time of growing disparity between and within nations, they will be held accountable for their misuse of the goods of the earth (69).

Moreover, it enunciates reform principles that would go far in eliminating the roots of social conflict and disparity: land reform, worker co-management and the dignity of work (67, 68, 71). Herein lie the seeds of the future encyclical *Laborem Exercens*. This section maintains the tradition rather than develops it. Because of its sensitivity to the cultural dimension, however, it suggests alternate visions of ownership.

Chapter 4: THE POLITICAL COMMUNITY

Growing aspirations for political freedom and participation mark the modern political arena. At the same time, the Church is aware of the continuing repression of such desires among most of the peoples of the planet.

Faithful to its earlier teaching on cultural pluralism and its anthropology, the Church acknowledges the rights of all to choose their own forms of government, but these governments must work for the common good and not usurp the functions of the various communities that comprise the state (74).

Disagreeing with both the extreme right and left, the Church sees the state as a necessary element in any society, which will not wither away. It has an essential role in creating "the sum total of all those conditions of social life which enable individuals, families, and organizations to achieve complete and efficacious fulfilment." Those who are familiar with Catholic social teaching will see in this quotation the bi-polar aspects of the principle of "subsidiarity": groups and individuals must be encouraged to contribute to the common good; at the same time, because of their limitations, state intervention may be necessary.

This section stresses the importance of political vocation. It urges Christians with the talent to train for it and work at it, so that the common good is realized (75). But they must keep in mind the distinction "between the activities of Christians, acting individually or collectively in their own name as citizens guided by the dictates of a Christian conscience, and their activity acting along with their pastors in the name of the Church" (76).

This is an important distinction, for political action and involvement in the concrete, contingent, realities of the political world will often suggest alternate plans for solving problems. "It happens rather frequently and legitimately so that some of the faithful, with no less sincerity, will see the problem quite differently" (43).

The recent debates in the United States on peace and in Canada on unemployment are such examples. In the former case, all want peace but not all will agree on the means to achieve it. In the latter instance, economists have offered many different strategies to deal with unemployment.

In looking to the Church for help in forming their conscience, the laity must understand that their pastors may not have a "ready answer to every problem that arises (even every grave problem)" (43). Lay persons must learn to act on their own in these matters, even independently of the Church and the political community (75).

Whenever the fundamental rights of humanity and its salvation are at stake, however, the Church claims the right and duty of "passing moral judgment even in matters relating to politics" (75). The American bishops' pastoral letter on nuclear armaments and the Canadian bishops' reflections on the economy were controversial, but in my opinion, were faithful to the vision of *Gaudium et Spes*.

Chapter 5: FOSTERING OF PEACE AND THE ESTABLISHMENT OF A COMMUNITY OF NATIONS

It is to the credit of the Council that it ended its deliberations not just with a condemnation of war, but with a theology of peace and an injuction to rethink conflict resolution by war (80).

While it urges the nations of the world to move in this direction, it also affirms the rights of self-defence, as long as all peaceful means have been exhausted. In fact, this section is a re-statement of the just war theory.

Sanctioned through the ages, this theory has now been called into question by the new possibilities of war. Total war, especially by nuclear means, falls outside the principles governing a just war. The Council condemns it unequivocally: "every act of war directed to the indiscriminate destruction of whole cities or vast areas with their inhabitants is a crime against God and man, and merits firm and unequivocal condemnation" (80).

While it still sees military service as a legitimate service to one's country, it also supports those who espouse non-violent approaches to self-defence and upholds conscientious objection (79).

Preparation for total war can also do harm: "As long as extravagant sums of money are poured into the development of new weapons, it is impossible to devote adequate aid in tackling the misery which prevails at the present day in the world" (81).

Disarmament, then, is imperative; it must be bi-lateral and mutually verifiable (82).

Being realistic, the Church can envisage the worst, where the only peace in the world "will be the dread peace of death" (82). It tempers this dark possibility, however, with an unfailing sense of hope that will continue to preach the Gospel of peace and justice in season and out.

Finally, the document proposes that the solution is not a balance of terror but the pursuit of justice. This quest requires the development of new international structures and an eventual trans-national form of authority to look after the universal common good (85).

The momentous challenge of working for world peace requires the Church to work also for unity among the Churches; this would be a hopeful sign that all peoples can finally be united in peace and fraternity (92). The witness of unity (Jn 17:2) and the witness of charity (Jn 13:35) are therefore indispensible ways to proclaim the Good News and to anticipate the harmony of the world to come (93).

Christological Perspective

In his seminal work *Christ and Culture*,[16] H. Richard Niebuhr depicts the Catholic stance vis-à-vis culture as one of "Christ above culture." His own preferred model is that of "Christ transforming Culture."

It is my thesis that *Gaudium et Spes* marks a transition to the transformational model. This is evident in the turn to the historical, in the growing consciousness of the Church's responsibility for the world, and also in an integral view of evangelization. At the same time, as noted in the commentary on chapter 3, the relationship between human progress and Christian salvation is left in an ambiguous state. ✓

The Synod of 1971 came closest to a solution by stating that "participation in the transformation of the world is a constitutive dimension of the preaching of the Gospel."[17] However, the word "constitutive" has itself been questioned. The International Theological Commission has interpreted the phrase to mean "an integral and not essential part."[18] Bishop Alex Carter, who was present as a Canadian representative, disagrees and claims that it means "essential," a necessary condition for the full proclamation of the Gospel.[19]

We cannot resolve this major theological question here. A solution probably lies in further reflection on the Paschal Mystery—something that *Gaudium et Spes* inaugurates.[20] ✓

Ecclesiological Dimensions

Much is made of the shift in understanding of the nature of the Church fostered by Vatican II. *Lumen Gentium* begins with the "People of God" model, then complements it with a "hierarchical" perspective. The documents also mention the "Body of Christ" and the "Church as Sacrament."

Reflection on *Gaudium et Spes* reveals an operational definition of the Church as "Servant-Healer."[21] This is revealed in its concern for collaboration with all people of good will, in its recognition of the proper autonomy of secular society, and the theme of "solidarity" that marked the introduction.

The theologian Avery Dulles has challenged the adequacy of these models.[22] In an article entitled "Imaging the Church for the 1980's," he writes that the Church would be more adequately described as a "community of disciples in the Lord Jesus Christ." He claims this model would save the best insights of the other main ecclesial images. In particular, he is concerned that the servant model tends to define the Church as:

> Wholly in function of its social or humanitarian contribution. Some, misled by the triumphalistic rhetoric, have imagined that it was the Church's task to solve all social, political, and economic problems, and have subsequently become disillusioned about the Church's lack of qualifications for this role...The dissatisfaction occasioned by such efforts has posed with new urgency the demand to clarify the Church's relationship with the socio-political order.[23]

In *Gaudium et Spes* the Church is very clear in announcing that "Christ did not bequeath to the Church a mission in the political, economic, or social order" (42). Here the meaning of the word "Church" is ambiguous: the whole document is at pains to get the laity involved in transforming the world. They do have a definite mission in this regard—their principal mission is to work at the transformation of the world, and they are the Church.

Despite these ambiguities, we have a new understanding of the Church. This amounts to a new paradigm, to use a favourite word of the philosophy of science.[24]

According to John O'Malley, this paradigm can be summarized as "the basic intuition underlying aggiornamento, that with all sorts of qualifications, religion had to meet the 'needs of the times'."[25] This view encouraged a rhetoric of "great expectations" that has been and is dangerous for the Church's renewal. O'Malley points out that:

> Especially in *Gaudium et Spes*, it held out the hopes for a world in which justice and peace would reign and in which religion and technology would cooperate for a more humane environment. The optimism of this document has often been noted. It helped create a vision of hope in a world receptive to such a message. But visions of hope, unless somehow soon realized, tend after a short while to be forgotten or to turn sour. It seems to be true, unfortunately, that the "rhetoric of reproach" has more staying power.[26]

This optimism is mitigated by the recognition of the darkest possibilities latent in nuclear war. Ultimately, I believe, it is better to err on the side of hope than to give in to the despair over the vicissitudes of history.

O'Malley summarizes the intuition of Vatican II about this as follows:

31

The persistent Catholic impulse to reconcile "nature and grace" is, when raised to the level of social institutions, an impulse to reconcile the Church with human culture in all its positive dimensions—with sin excepted, and the Gospel affirmed. In that sense the Council, for all its daring, moved solidly in line with the Catholic tradition...The Church is fully incorporated into human history and changes that take place there deeply affect it. This is what the Council saw, and that perception is perhaps its best legacy.[27]

Ecclesial Impact of Gaudium et Spes

What evidence, then is there of the impact of *Schema 13* twenty years later?

Bernard Lambert, O.P., a Canadian theologian and peritus at Vatican II, has documented the structural changes:

> The whole second part of *Gaudium et Spes* has been translated into institutions, first in the Roman Curia and often in the Church at large. The first chapter on the family has given rise to the Pontifical Council for the family, the second on culture to the Pontifical Council for culture, the chapter on socio-economic life was forwarded by "Populorum Progressio" of Paul VI and by "Laborem Exercens" of Pope John Paul. The chapter on peace gave birth to the Pontifical Commission on justice and peace. The Pontifical Council "Cor Unum" also stemmed from the Constitution.[28]

In the Americas the effects have been substantial. In Latin America, for example, Medellin and Pueblo have become familiar names because of the pastoral reflections issued from these synods. The documents they produced basically form a dialogue with, on the one hand, Vatican II, in particular *Gaudium et Spes*, and, on the other, the reality of Latin America.

Latin America

Juan Carlos Scannone, S.J., an Argentinian theologian, identifies three pastoral trends emanating from this document. The first is based on the "two planes theory." This model holds that salvation history and human temporal progress are distinct but related realities, that the mission of the Church is primarily focussed on changing hearts and informing consciences of the laity who in turn will work at social transformation.

This model is faithful to the texts of *Gaudium et Spes* that stress the rightful autonomy of the secular world, the role of the laity in temporal affairs, and the lack of a mission in the temporal world. But, because it tends to be individualistic, it deals poorly with structural realities such as the economic system of capitalism, and tends to ignore the traditional cultures of the region. It also downplays the prophetic role of the hierarchical Church.[29]

A second pastoral approach is found in certain schools of liberation theology. In this view:

The evangelization of culture will have to experience first the liberation of the oppressed cultures, which in turn will be conditioned by the liberating transformation of the labour system and of the social power. This transformation is conceived along socialist lines.[30]

This method is Marxist in orientation and uses in particular a class analysis as a basis for cultural investigations. It is realistic in assessing the power structure in place, although voluntaristic in asserting that communities can shape their reality and change the oppressive situation.

The "popular religion" of Latin America has posed a problem for this school. Trying to be faithful to the preferential option for the poor, some maintain that popular culture should be the focus of evangelization. Others, assuming that the indigenous and hybrid cultures of Latin America are doomed to extinction, stress the evangelization of the modern working sectors of society.

A third trend is culturally focussed. It sees new cultural reality blending the indigenous and Iberian cultures in Latin America. It also acknowledges that evangelization played an important role in the development of this culture. Today it wants to evangelize, "starting from the religious dimension, and through the mediation of ethics,...reach all the other dimensions of human life and dialogue."[31] Cultural anthropologists would view this approach as akin to their own revitalization theory. In other words, no cultural renewal can take place without a religious renewal.[32]

Scannone concludes his description by stating that "the evangelization of culture should take as a starting point the inculturation of the Gospel within popular culture."[33]

The United States
The American bishops' recent pastoral letter, *The Challenge of Peace*, is a concrete example of the influence of *Gaudium et Spes*. Basically, the conciliar document provided the rationale for such political deliberations and recommended a revision of our attitudes towards war.

According to Bryan Hehir, "[On] three ecclesiological themes, the place of the Church in the world, its style of presence and its perspective, the contributions of the Pastoral Constitution directly shaped how the American bishops pursued their task."[34] The place of the Church is in the world, safeguarding the transcendental dimension of the human person; its style is dialogue; and its perspective is to read the "signs of the times" in light of the Gospel.

What was remarkable about the process and the product of the American bishops was the fidelity to this vision of the pastoral constitution. The crisis of the nuclear arms race provided the "sign" that required a response. The style of hearings and the publication of drafts, eliciting responses from different sources, exemplified "dialogue" in action. And the "place" of the Church provided the motivation.

While the pastoral letter—both its content and courage—will stand as a landmark in Church teaching on the issue of war and peace, I believe the style of producing such documents will be equally lasting. This could be a North American contribution to Church praxis in general.

At the same time, some questions remain. Does the Church have to consult everyone before making a statement about peace? Does not the wide consultation process water down the prophetic dimension?

Canada: Social Ecumenism

In terms of generating interest in society, the recent pastoral letter of the Canadian bishops, *Ethical Reflections on the Economic Crisis*, was a huge success. While some have questioned the process, a close reading of the document shows that the bishops had hoped to spark just such a response, to get the whole country involved in the solutions that can only come over time and with much hard work.

Their style was prophetic, but also encouraged an ongoing dialogue on the problems the paper discussed.

This document is typical of the social teaching of the Canadian Catholic Church since Vatican II. While Vatican II did not inaugurate a tradition of social concern, it did accelerate it.[35] The Canadian Catholic Conference of Bishops set up its social action commission in 1947. Beginning in 1956 it began a tradition of issuing yearly social statements on the occasion of Labour Day. In recent years, this tradition has been maintained, but not tied to a set date. For example, the ethical reflections document came out on New Year's Day, 1983.

During the years after Vatican II, significant changes took place in the pastoral letters. There has always been, and still is, a great gap between papal pronouncements and the practice of the faithful. Perhaps as a response to *Octogesimo Adveniens* (addressed to a Canadian cardinal), the Church's teaching became more specific, action-oriented, and gave rise to what many others and I consider the unique Canadian contribution to Church life—ecumenical collaboration on social issues.

In addition to calling for the setting up of Catholic institutions to promote justice and peace, the *Pastoral Constitution on the Church in the Modern World* also encouraged ecumenical efforts in the same areas. The Catholic Church in Canada did both. It set up, for example, the Canadian Catholic Organization for Development and Peace, and also joined many ecumenical coalitions to address national and international social issues. An unpublished study commissioned by the World Council of Churches concluded that no country in the world was as advanced in this ecumenical effort as Canada.[36]

But ecumenism has not filtered down to the regional and parish levels. As we look to the future, and across the Americas, the great task is to involve the laity in the social ministry and have them assume their rightful place and mission of transforming the world.

Future Consideration

The late Karl Rahner is certainly correct in saying that the Church has entered a new era.[37] The first epoch of the Church was a short one: the history of Jewish Christianity. The second epoch was the predominately European phase. But at Vatican II, for the first time we see a global Catholic Church in embryo. For the first time, there were bishops from all areas of the world who were indigenous. The future will then witness a greater desire to enculturate the Gospel. To do this we could combine the "cultural" approach of the Latin Americans, the "dialogue" style of the Americans, and the "social ecumenism" of the Canadian Churches.

Other continents and cultures will no doubt make their unique contributions to the incarnation of *Gaudium et Spes*. Together, we can become Catholic in the fullest sense.

Notes

1. A.P. Flannery, O.P., ed., *The Documents of Vatican II* (New York: Pillar Books, 1975), hereafter cited as *Gaudium et Spes* with the article number.
2. Quoted in an editorial of the *National Catholic Reporter*, Oct. 21, 1983, 12.
3. John O'Malley, S.J., "Developments, Reforms, and Two Great Reformations: Towards a Historical Assessment of Vatican II," *Theological Studies*, 44 (1983), 373–406.
4. Karl Rahner, S.J., "Towards a Fundamental Interpretation of Vatican II," *Theological Studies*, 40 (1979), 716–27.
5. Cardinal Suenens is generally credited with initiating this "ad extra" debate.
6. For a discussion of the mission theology of Colossians and Ephesians, see Donald Senior, C.P., and Carroll Stuhlmueller, C.P., *The Biblical Foundations for Mission* (Maryknoll, N.Y.: 1983), 191–210.
7. For an excellent overview of the status questions, see Bonaventure Kloppenburg, O.F.M., *Christian Salvation and Human Temporal Progress* (Chicago: Fransiscan Herald Press, 1979).
8. Senior and Stuhlmeuller, *The Biblical Foundations for Mission*, 208.
9. The best illustration of this shift of thinking is to be found in *Octogesimo Adveniens*. It contains the famous text that has stimulated pastoral reflection: "It is up to Christian communities to analyze with objectivity the situation which is proper to their own country, to shed on it the light of the Gospel's unalterable words, and to draw principles for reflection, norms of judgment, and directives of action from the social teaching of the Church." Apostolic letter of Paul VI, May 14, 1971, *The Pope Speaks*, 16 (1971), 137–64.
10. Vatican Congregation for Catholic Education, "Educational Guidance in Human Love," *Origins*, 13, no. 27 (1983), 449, 451–61.
11. H. Carrier, "Understanding Cultures: The Ultimate Challenge?" unpublished paper presented at the Notre Dame Symposium on *Gaudium et Spes*, Nov. 21–23, 1983, 3.
12. Bernard Lonergan, *Method in Theology* (New York: Seabury Press, 1979), xi, 124, 301.
13. Carrier, "Understanding Cultures," 5.

14. *Ibid.*, 6.

15. For a thorough missiological discussion of this problematic, see Charles H. Kraft, *Christianity in Culture* (Maryknoll, N.Y.: Orbis, 1979), especially receptor-oriented revelation, 169.

16. H.R. Niebuhr, *Christ and Culture* (New York: Harper Torchbooks, 1951).

17. Synod of Bishops (Rome, 1971), *Justice in the World* (Washington, D.C.: National Conference of Catholic Bishops, 1972), 34.

18. Kloppenburg, *Christian Salvation and Human Temporal Progress*, 94.

19. For a discussion of this phrase, see Charles Murphy, "Action for Justice as Constitutive of the Preaching of the Gospel: What Did the 1971 Synod Mean?" *Theological Studies*, 44 (1983), 298–311.

20. *Gaudium et Spes*, nos. 3, 10, 13, 22, 27, 38, 39, 45.

21. Avery Dulles, *Models of the Church* (Garden City, N.J.: Doubleday, 1978), 95–108.

22. *Ibid.*, 5.

23. O'Malley, "Developments, Reforms, and Two Great Reformations," 373–406.

24. *Ibid.*, 392.

25. *Ibid.*, 393.

26. *Ibid.*, 397.

27. *Ibid.*, 406.

28. Bernard Lambert, O.P., *Gaudium et Spes Yesterday and Today*, unpublished paper, Notre Dame, Nov. 21–23, 1983, 5.

29. Juan Carlos Scannone, S.J., *The Influence of Gaudium et Spes on the Issues of the Evangelization of Culture in Latin America: Evangelization, Liberation, and Popular Culture*, unpublished paper, Notre Dame, Nov. 21–23, 1983, 7–9.

30. *Ibid.*, 9–13.

31. *Ibid.*, 13-22.

32. For a case study close to home see, for example, Anthony F.C. Wallace, *The Death and Rebirth of the Seneca* (New York: Random House, 1972).

33. Scannone, *The Influence of Gaudium et Spes*, 18.

34. J. Bryan Hehir, *From the Pastoral Constitution of Vatican II to the Challenge of Peace: Continuity and Development*, unpublished paper, Notre Dame, Nov. 21–23, 1983, 8.

35. I am indebted to Bishop Remi De Roo for the overview of the development of the Canadian Catholic social teaching presented in *The Economy, Culture and Gospel Values: Church Dialogue with the Economy*, unpublished paper, Notre Dame, Nov. 21–23, 1983.

36. John Lucal, S.J., *Coalitions for Social Ecumenism: The Canadian Story.* This study, completed in 1980, has never been published.

37. Rahner, "Towards a Fundamental Interpretation of Vatican II," 718–725.

Decree on Ecumenism

Unitatis Redintegratio

W. MACBEATH BROWN

The Second Vatican Council's *Decree on Ecumenism, Unitatis Redintegratio,* has many important theological insights—such as the Catholic Church's acceptance of partial blame for Christian divisions; the asking of forgiveness and offering of pardon for those divisions; the recognition of the need for reform at all levels of Church life, even in the way magisterial teaching has been formulated; the affirmation that unity does not mean uniformity; and the brief but fervent call to all Christians to work together for social justice and peace.

This paper cannot deal with all of these; it does try, however, to cover what is of lasting importance in the decree. It will follow three themes evident throughout the document: the role of the Holy Spirit in the life of the Church, the role of every member of the Church in the work of greater Christian unity, and the idea and experience of the Church, the reality into which the Spirit brings every baptized Christian. They were not chosen arbitrarily. There is an obvious theological connection between them: all the major teachings of the *Decree on Ecumenism* are expressions of these three interrelated themes.

Several reasons encourage this approach. First, the decree is one of the most important of the Council texts, more closely related than others to the very purpose of the Council—the renewal and reform of the Church and the restoration of Christian unity. Second, because it is one of the shorter and more readable texts of the Council, it is more accessible to the whole membership of the Church. Third, unfortunately, like so much of the Second Vatican Council's teaching, the *Decree on Ecumenism* has simply not been received well enough yet by the whole Church. For only a few in the Church is ecumenism a priority twenty years after. Fourth, if one believes that the future of Christianity as a viable religious and spiritual force for all peoples consists in ecumenical unity, then there is an urgency for us, as Roman Catholics, to renew our commitment to Christian unity as urged by the Council Fathers. And finally, the *Decree on Ecumenism* can be studied alone, without constant reference to other Vatican II texts, partly because of its very purpose—a call to work to restore the Church's unity—and partly because it contains in its own text, *en résumé*, the major ideas of the other principal Council texts on the Church, the Word of God and the liturgy.

THE ROLE OF THE HOLY SPIRIT IN THE LIFE OF THE CHURCH

The decree emphasizes the role of the Holy Spirit to a degree that may have surprised Western Latin Roman Catholics twenty years ago, steeped in a post-Tridentine, neo-scholastic theology. This theology emphasized the power of all the institutionalized manifestations of the Church's life, that is, a monolithic and universal immediacy of the vicariate of Christ to members of the Church. The definition of Vatican I concerning petrine primacy and infallibility was only the logical and extreme development of this unbalanced theology. Such a theology was inevitably to the detriment of a proper and balanced place given to the role of the Holy Spirit.

The most comprehensive and most beautiful expression of the role of the Holy Spirit in the life of the Church comes near the beginning of the first chapter of the *Decree on Ecumenism*, entitled "Catholic Principles on Ecumenism":

> It is the Holy Spirit, dwelling in those who believe and pervading and ruling over the entire Church, who brings about that wonderful communion of the faithful and joins them together so intimately in Christ that he is the principle of the Church's unity. By distributing various kinds of spiritual gifts and ministries he enriches the Church of Jesus Christ with different functions "in order to equip the saints for the work of service, so as to build up the body of Christ" (Eph 4:12).[1]

The decree goes on immediately to describe the foundational functions given by the Spirit, mediating the faith of every believer in Christ Jesus of all times. These are the teaching, ruling and sanctifying exercised by the apostles and their successors. Here again, the text mentions the Holy Spirit specifically:

> It is through the faithful preaching of the Gospel by the Apostles and their successors—the bishops with Peter's successor at their head—through their administering the sacraments, and through their governing in love, that Jesus Christ wishes his people to increase, under the action of the Holy Spirit.

38

Two short paragraphs later, the decree states:

> This is the sacred mystery of the unity of the Church, in Christ and through Christ, with the Holy Spirit energizing its various functions. The highest exemplar and source of this mystery is the unity, in the Trinity of Persons, of one God, the Father and the Son in the Holy Spirit.

"*In* the Holy Spirit" rather than "*and* the Holy Spirit" emphasizes the Spirit as the bond of love between the Father and the Son; it also makes the whole trinitarian formula resemble most closely the World Council of Churches expression in its *Statement on Unity* in 1961: "The love of the Father and the Son *in* the unity of the Holy Spirit is the source and goal of the unity...in the Church of Jesus Christ..."

After speaking of the duty for Catholics to renew and reform their own "household of faith" and also to recognize and esteem "the riches of Christ" present in those separated from them, the decree goes on to say, "nor should we forget that anything wrought by the grace of the Holy Spirit in the hearts of our separated brethren can contribute to our own edification" (4). Once again, this is a very precise and correct theological expression: our "first contact" with, our "entry point" to the Father and the Son is by and through the Holy Spirit.[2]

Near the beginning of the second chapter of the decree, after an insistent description of the Church's need both for renewal and reform, the text continues:

> There can be no ecumenism worthy of the name without interior conversion...We should therefore pray to the Holy Spirit for the grace to be genuinely self-denying, humble, gentle in the service of others.

This prayer to the Holy Spirit was not a popular, wide-spread practice among Roman Catholics in the early 1960's; they were much more used to praying to or through Holy Mary the Virgin, Mother of God, or some other saints.

A third reference is in the last section of the decree before its conclusion, where the Council considers the particularities of the Protestant ecclesial communities of the West, separated from communion with the Roman See. The text signals out, seemingly in praise, their "love and reverence—almost a cult—of Holy Scripture" (21). The Council continues, a few lines beyond, in a very interesting trinitarian and christological expression:

> While invoking the Holy Spirit [the separated brothers and sisters] seek in these very scriptures God as he speaks to them in Christ, the one whom the prophets foretold, the Word of God made flesh for us (21).

This text was one of a score of passages Pope Paul VI altered before the final vote on the decree; in the final draft before the papal modification, the text had read: "As the Holy Spirit moves them, they find in these very Scriptures God speaking to them in Christ."

The papal modification of this passage was done to safeguard the role of the Magisterium in interpreting Scripture.

The final passages of the decree are rich in evocations of the Holy Spirit—four references in two short paragraphs. The first is the most important for our study:

> This sacred Council firmly hopes that the initiatives of the sons of the Catholic Church, joined with those of the separated brethren, will go forward, without obstructing the ways of divine Providence, and without prejudging the future inspirations of the Holy Spirit (24).

This phrase, "without prejudging the future inspirations of the Holy Spirit," is particularly instructive in helping us appreciate the quality of references to the Holy Spirit in the decree. The Holy Spirit is the ultimate and absolute "free spirit"; we simply do not know where and when the Spirit will "blow" and what newness of life this "moving" will call us to. The Council documents, including the *Decree on Ecumenism*, never oppose the Holy Spirit and the visible, institutional Church. But the *Decree on Ecumenism* in particular, perhaps more than any other single text of Vatican II, certainly more than any papal or conciliar text since the Reformation in the West, emphasizes the role of the Holy Spirit as the initiator in the triune God's mysterious, gentle action, intervening in our human existence to liberate and fulfil it. This role of the Holy Spirit is always unpredictable, uncontrollable and future-oriented, always "blowing" towards a "renewal and reform of the face of the earth," including Christ's one and only Catholic Church. This deeper realization of the role of the Holy Spirit was crucial to any true renewal and reform of the Church—it meant that the visible structures and ministries, laws, customs and courts could not always set the rule. To use a theological insight of Vatican II (which we will refer to at greater length further on), one could say that the divine Spirit-given graces of Gospel, ecclesial inspirations, leadership, patience and perseverance subsist in the institutional Church but are never totally identical with it. This profound theological realization was necessary to restore to all members of the People of God their personal, active role in and responsibility for the Church of Christ, first and foremost its unity.

THE ROLE AND RESPONSIBILITY OF EVERY MEMBER OF THE CATHOLIC CHURCH TO WORK FOR THE UNITY OF ALL CHRISTIANS
Another area of radical renewal, some would say authentic reform, proclaimed by the *Decree on Ecumenism* and crucial in an evaluation

twenty years after, is the call to all members of the Catholic Church to play "an active and intelligent" role in the ecumenical movement, the work of promoting greater unity among Christians. This call to the whole Church comes naturally as our next consideration after looking at the role of the Holy Spirit; often the Holy Spirit and the whole People of God are mentioned together.

INTRODUCTION AND CHAPTER 1 OF THE DECREE

In the introduction to the whole decree, the text affirms:

> The Sacred Council...moved by a desire for the restoration of unity among all the followers of Christ,...wishes to set before all Catholics guidelines, helps and methods, by which they too can respond to the grace of this divine call (1).

After describing the Spirit-given foundational unity of the Church of Christ, and the historical ruptures of that unity (2 and 3), the decree turns to a more practical consideration of the ecumenical movement:

> Today, in many parts of the world, under the influence of the grace of the Holy Spirit, many efforts are being made in prayer, word and action to attain that fullness of unity which Jesus Christ desires. The sacred Council exhorts, therefore, all the Catholic faithful to recognize the signs of the times and to take an active and intelligent part in the work of ecumenism (4).

The decree enumerates five principal areas of ecumenical action: avoidance of all polemics about our brothers and sisters separated from us, theological dialogue between competent persons, common humanitarian works, common prayer, and renewal and reform of all followers of Christ (4). That all these areas of ecumenical action can involve any member of the Catholic Church is absolutely clear:

> Such actions, when they are carried out by the Catholic faithful with prudent patience and under the attentive guidance of their bishops, promote justice and truth, concord and collaboration,...love and unity (4).

The decree proceeds with some almost astonishing affirmations — astonishing, in any case, for Latin Roman Catholics in the early 1960's:

> Catholics must assuredly be concerned for their separated brethren,...making the first approaches towards them. But their [that is, of all Catholics] primary duty is to make a careful and honest appraisal of whatever needs to be renewed and done in the Catholic household itself...Every Catholic must aim therefore at Christian perfection and, each according to his station, play his part, that the Church...may daily be more purified and renewed...While preserving unity in essentials, let everyone in the Church, according to the office entrusted to him, preserve

41

a proper freedom in the various forms of spiritual life...and even in the theological elaborations of revealed truth....[Thus] they [that is, all Catholics] will be giving ever richer expression to the authentic catholicity and apostolicity of the Church (4).

This last paragraph ("While preserving unity in essentials...") in particular could leave all Catholics truly "surprised by joy" in its confident call to each one of them to action, freedom, and discerning essentials and non-essentials.

Having thus described every Catholic's responsibility and ordered freedom to foster the renewal and reform of the Church, the Council goes on:

On the other hand, Catholics must gladly acknowledge and esteem the truly Christian endowments for our common heritage which are to be found among our separated brethren...Nor should we [that is, all Catholics] forget that anything wrought by the grace of the Holy Spirit in the hearts of our separated brethren can contribute to our own edification" (4).

The decree then ends this first chapter:

This sacred Council is gratified to note that the participation by the Catholic faithful in ecumenical work is growing daily. It commends this work to the bishops everywhere in the world for their diligent promotion and prudent guidance (4).

It would indeed be difficult to imagine a more balanced statement than this one in truly Catholic doctrine and theology. It affirms every Catholic's real though limited freedom and responsibility in the matter of renewal and reform of the whole Church under episcopal leadership, specifically to promote the greater unity of the Church. At last full Christian adulthood is recognized in all the Catholic faithful. Ecumenical action is the responsibility of every one of them, not just of some specialized experts; the first steps in dialogue and other ecumenical work will in fact most often be initiated by lay persons. And the bishops must not only prudently guide all this work for greater Christian unity, but also diligently promote it.

CHAPTERS 2 AND 3

This enthusiasm of the Council was of such importance as to be carried over, immediately, to the beginning of the second chapter of the decree, "The Practice of Ecumenism." This re-emphasized the call of all Catholics to participate in the ecumenical movement, first and foremost through the renewal and reform of their own Catholic Church:

The concern for restoring unity involves the whole Church, faithful and clergy alike. It extends to everyone, according to the talent of each, whether it be exercised in daily Christian living or in theological and historical studies. This concern itself [for restoring unity, involving the whole Church] already reveals to some extent the bond of brotherhood existing among all Christians and it leads toward full and perfect unity (5).

After explaining further what it means by renewal and reform of the Church necessarily accompanied by interior conversion, the Council concludes:

The faithful should remember that they promote union among Christians better, that indeed they live it better, when they try to live holier lives...This change of heart and holiness of life [that is, of all the faithful], along with public and private prayer for the unity of Christians, should be regarded as the soul of the whole ecumenical movement, and merits the name, "spiritual ecumenism" (7, 8).

The rest of chapter 2 speaks of prayer for unity, rare situations of worship in common, serious study of our separated brethren's outlook, and theological dialogues. The implication is that all Catholics can participate in those aspects that might be called "ongoing ecumenism"; competency is the only norm of participation:

It is allowable, indeed desirable, that Catholics should join in prayer with their separated brethren...for the grace of unity...worship in common is not...a means to be used indiscriminately for the restoration of unity among Christians (8).
Catholics who already have a proper grounding need to acquire a more adequate understanding of the respective doctrines of our separated brethren...Most valuable...are meetings of the two sides—especially for discussion of theological problems—where each can treat with the other on an equal footing, provided that those who take part...are truly competent (9).

Chapter 3 has relatively much fewer references to the work of greater Christian unity by all members of the Catholic Church. What references it has consistently maintain the same point of view as in chapters 1 and 2—it is the work of the whole Church:

It is earnestly recommended that Catholics avail themselves more often of the spiritual riches of the Eastern Fathers...Everyone should recognize that it is of supreme importance to understand, venerate, preserve and foster the rich liturgical and spiritual heritage of the Eastern Churches in order faithfully to preserve the fullness of Christian tradition, and to bring about reconciliation between Eastern and Western Christians (15).
To the pastors and faithful of the Catholic Church, [this sacred Council] commends close relations with those [Eastern Christians] no longer living in the East, but far from their homeland, so that friendly collaboration with them may increase (18).

The Council begins its conclusion to the entire decree with a last reference to the ecumenical work incumbent upon the whole membership of the Catholic Church:

> This sacred Council urges the faithful to abstain from any frivolous or imprudent zeal, for these can cause harm to true progress towards unity. Their ecumenical activity cannot be other than fully and sincerely Catholic, that is, loyal to the truth we have received from the Apostles and the Fathers, and in harmony with the faith which the Catholic Church has always professed...This sacred Council firmly hopes that the initiatives of the sons of the Catholic Church, joined with those of the separated brethren, will go forward (24).

SPECIAL CATEGORIES OF PERSONS IN ECUMENICAL WORK

Only two passages in the decree refer to a specific ecumenical role of ordained ministers other than the overseeing role of bishops mentioned several times throughout the document. The first states:

> There can be no ecumenism worthy of the name without interior conversion....We should therefore pray to the Holy Spirit for the grace to be genuinely self-denying, humble, gentle in the service of others...This exhortation is directed especially to those raised to sacred orders in order that the mission of Christ may be continued. He came among us "not to be served, but to serve" (Mt 20:28), (7).

The second passage occurs further in the same chapter, "The Practice of Ecumenism":

> Sacred theology...must be taught with due regard for the ecumenical point of view...It is important that future pastors and priests should have mastered a theology that has been carefully elaborated in this way [that is, with an ecumenical point of view] and not polemically, especially in what concerns the relations of separated brethren with the Catholic Church. For it is upon the formation which priests receive that so largely depends the necessary instruction and spiritual formation of the faithful and of religious (10).

In both these cases it is clear that all ordained ministry exists as such in order to serve the whole membership of the Catholic Church. One very important aspect of that service is to teach the Gospel, always with an ecumenical spirit and attitude in mind.

Only one other passage in the whole decree signals out a restricted category of persons to play a special role in the great work of ecumenism. Many commentators would claim that the following passage is the most important theological breakthrough of the entire *Decree on Ecumenism* in what it says about the subject of theologians, that is, doctrinal truths.

The text in which the decree refers to theologians follows immediately upon the passage just discussed about the "ecumenically minded" theological formation of future pastors and priests.

The decree goes on:

> The manner and order in which Catholic belief is expressed should in no way become an obstacle to dialogue with our brethren (11).

In doing this, Catholic doctrine must be "clearly presented in its entirety" to avoid any sort of "false irenicism" (11), and must be explained as thoroughly as possible so that "our separated brethren can also really understand it" (11). Immediately following this is the key paragraph that we referred to as truly a theological breakthrough:

> Furthermore, in ecumenical dialogue, Catholic theologians, standing fast by the teaching of the Church yet searching together with separated brethren into the divine mysteries, should do so with love for the truth, with charity, and with humility. When comparing doctrines with one another, they should remember that in Catholic doctrine there exists an order or "hierarchy" of truths, since they vary in their relation to the foundation of the Christian faith. Thus the way will be opened whereby this kind of "fraternal rivalry" [in comparing doctrines] will incite all to a deeper realization and a clearer expression of the unfathomable riches of Christ (11).

For Latin Roman Catholics of the early 1960's, this passage was indeed "good news" in the truest sense of the Gospel. Very few of them would ever actually read this passage—and this is probably so even twenty years later—but its spirit has filtered through in indirect ways, especially through the reform of the liturgy and of preaching. Most Catholics in the 1980's know that the Lord's Day celebration of the Eucharist is the heart of their faith and ecclesial life, precisely because it celebrates the central truth of their faith, the triune God's saving presence and action in our human existence. The "one thing necessary" is to adore the Father, through the Son, through his death and resurrection and coming again for us, and in the Holy Spirit, who is in us since our baptism. All the other sacraments, all the sacramentals, all the other dogmas, devotions, practices, penitences, venerations—all are at least secondary if not less in "relation to the foundation of Christian faith."

The text speaks of Catholic theologians without any allusion to clerical status. In other works, the competence already mentioned by the decree itself is the only criterion that counts, in whatever area of ecumenical work. Even if many individual bishops at the Council had male clerics in mind when thinking of "Catholic theologians," that is not what the conciliar document says. This is important; in the following twenty years, many lay theologians, men and women, have been active,

45

creative members of national or international theological dialogues. This is particularly true in Canada of the national Anglican-Roman Catholic and United (Reformed)-Roman Catholic Dialogues, both of which have produced several very significant theological statements.

Catholic theologians searching together with separated brethren into the divine mysteries must remember that in Catholic doctrine, there exists a hierarchy of truths. As one teaching of Vatican II, this expresses a deep desire for renewal of the Church, its life, its teaching, especially its way of teaching. For here, as in every other case of the Council's truly seminal insights, one can wonder to what degree any of them has affected the understanding and activity of the members of the Church. How much have all Catholics, including all ordained bishops, priests, deacons, really "received" the renewal and reform of the Church that Vatican II called for, encouraged and exhorted? We will return to this question in our conclusion.

THE CATHOLIC CHURCH

The idea of "the Church" and of "Churches" (local, particular) and of "ecclesial communities" in the *Decree on Ecumenism* could easily have been the sole subject of a study the length of this one. This paper will focus on what we consider to be original or renewed and to have borne the greatest fruit in the past two decades, and what promises to do so in the future.

One could summarize the decree's way of speaking of the Church as follows: there is one and only one Church of Christ; the one Church of Christ is the Catholic Church; the fullness of the Catholic Church subsists in the Roman Catholic Church, presided over by the bishop of Rome (hence "Roman") and the bishops throughout the world who are in communion with the bishop of Rome.

The decree tries briefly to describe the whole mystery of the "one and only" Church. It emphasizes the role of the Holy Spirit as the principle of the unity of the Church, visibly manifested especially in the presiding ministry of "the Apostles and their successors—the bishops with Peter's successor at their head" (2). It then goes on to describe the separation of "quite large communities...from full communion with the Catholic Church" and their consequent incomplete though real ecclesial reality. For Latin Roman Catholics of the early 1960's, these were powerful, positive, new affirmations indeed. It is worth recalling the key affirmations and the progression of thought, from consideration of individuals to consideration of ecclesial communities, in the conciliar text:

> Large communities became separated from full communion with the
> Catholic Church—for which, often enough, men of both sides were to

46

blame...the Catholic Church accepts them [those born into, baptized and nurtured in these communities today] with respect and affection as brothers. For men who believe in Christ and have been properly baptized are put into some, though imperfect, communion with the Catholic Church.

All who have been justified by faith in baptism are incorporated into Christ; they therefore have a right to be called Christians and with good reason are accepted as brothers by the children of the Catholic Church (3).

All the above statements certainly concern individual believers, though perhaps not all ecclesial communities. A transition seems to begin in the next paragraph:

Some, even very many, of the most significant elements and endowments which together go to build up and give life to the Church itself, can exist outside the visible boundaries of the Catholic Church: the written Word...grace; faith, hope and charity,...other interior gifts of the Holy Spirit, as well as visible elements [presumably ecclesial, communal]. All of these, which come from Christ and lead back to him, belong by right to the one Church of Christ (3).

The decree's recognition of the limited but real ecclesial nature of separated Christian communities is absolutely clear, and quite remarkable:

The brethren divided from us also carry out many liturgical actions....In ways that vary according to the condition of each Church or community, these liturgical actions most certainly can truly engender a life of grace and...can aptly give access to the communion of salvation....It follows that the separated Churches and communities as such, though we believe they suffer from defects, have been by no means deprived of significance and importance in the mystery of salvation. For the Spirit of Christ has not refrained from using them as means of salvation which derive their efficacy from the very fullness of grace and truth entrusted to the Catholic Church....Nevertheless, our separated brethren, whether considered as individuals or as communities and Churches, are not blessed with that unity which Jesus Christ wished (3).

The Council then goes on immediately to affirm the fullness of ecclesia in the Catholic Church alone:

For it is through Christ's Catholic Church alone, which is the universal help towards salvation, that the fullness of the means of salvation can be obtained. It was to the apostolic college alone, of which Peter is the head, that we believe that our Lord entrusted all the blessings of the New Covenant, in order to establish on earth the one Body of Christ (3).

The decree repeats this great affirmation of principle, with a special focus on the Church's unity:

The result [of ecumenical works] will be that, little by little,...all Christians will be gathered, in a common celebration of the Eucharist, into the unity of the one and only Church, which Christ bestowed on his Church from the beginning. This unity, we believe, subsists in the Catholic Church, as something she can never lose, and we hope that it will continue to increase until the end of time (4).

CONSEQUENCES OF THE IDEA OF "SUBSISTS IN"

The phrase "subsists in" was a truly seminal innovation on the part of the theologians who composed and reworked the drafts of the Vatican Council II. The phrase had already been used in the *Dogmatic Constitution on the Church* in a complementary passage to this one in the *Decree on Ecumenism*. It helps us understand the sense of the latter decree:

> This Church, constituted and organized as a society in the present world, subsists in the Catholic Church...governed by the successor of Peter and by the bishops in communion with him. Nevertheless, many elements of sanctification and of truth are found outside of its visible structure. Since these are gifts belonging to the Church of Christ, they are forces impelling towards Catholic unity (LG 8).

As these words make clear, this truly revolutionary new theological phrase allows a certain nuance of meaning: the first reality spoken of is truly present in the second reality, but it is not necessarily totally identical or co-extensive with it. This is so because we are not speaking of static immutable realities, but of evolving, developing, growing, dynamic realities. Neither the Catholic Church here and now nor the degree of Christian unity today is complete or fulfilled. This state of affairs seems to be clearly evoked in the way the above passage ends—with a hope that the Church's unity "will continue to increase."

The idea of an as-yet-imperfect fulfilment in the Catholic Church itself, as the unique Church of Christ, is clearly confirmed in two closely related passages. These were once again new and positive in the Catholic mentality of the early 1960's:

> For although the Catholic Church has been endowed with all divinely revealed truth and with all means of grace, yet its members fail to live by them with all the fervor that they should. As a result, the radiance of the Church's face shines less brilliantly in the eyes of our separated brethren and of the world at large, and the growth of God's kingdom is retarded (4).

It affirms the riches of Christ found outside the visible boundaries of the Catholic Church: "Whatever is truly Christian is never contrary to what genuinely belongs to the faith; indeed, it can always bring a more perfect realization of the very mystery of Christ and the Church" (4). The Council goes on to conclude:

48

Nevertheless, the divisions among Christians prevent the Church from realizing the fullness of catholicity proper to her in those of her sons...separated from full communion with her. Furthermore, the Church herself finds it more difficult to express in actual life her full catholicity in all its aspects (4).

With this statement, the Catholic Church went a long way towards being able to function practically as a "sister church" vis-à-vis at least the mainline Protestant Churches and the Churches of the East.

CHURCH AND CHURCHES

We now will focus on the question of Churches or ecclesial communities in the West. The West is chosen partly because our practical experience of the decree over the past twenty years is above all that of Western Christians; partly also because the decree is relatively uncomplicated and entirely positive about the ecclesial reality of the Churches of the East. At the risk of oversimplifying, the decree's judgment about the Eastern Churches can be summarized thus: these Churches are truly local Churches wherein the full mystery of the Church of Christ is present and manifested through a complete sacramental life, especially in and flowing out of the Eucharist presided over by the local Church's bishop or his delegated presbyterial ministers; the communions between these Churches, whether ancient, patriarchal, regional, national or ethnic, are true communions within the whole of the universal Church.

These Churches lack only one essential: the unique and universally exercised primatial petrine ministry of nurturing full communion among the communions and the Churches, a visible, efficacious ministry "willed by Christ the Lord" for Peter and his successors, historically the bishops of Rome, within the college of the apostles and their successors, all the bishops of the Catholic Church.

It is worth mentioning the relatively discreet way the *Decree on Ecumenism* refers to the petrine ministry. In explicit references to it (2–5), especially its origin, the immediate context includes a reference to Christ or the Holy Spirit as the ultimate initiator behind any petrine ministerial action. The very first reference to a petrine ministry recalls Scriptural passages upholding this: "with Jesus Christ Himself forever remaining the chief cornerstone (cf. Eph 2:20) and shepherd of our souls (cf. 1 Pet 2:25)." The absolute "rock" and pastor of the Church is Christ himself. Peter and his successors are "rocks" only in a secondary, subordinated, participatory way. The *Decree on Ecumenism* always refers to Peter and his successors collegially; they are always situated within the apostolic college (the apostles and their successors, the bishops) as part of this college, albeit at its head. This manner of speaking reflects the more balanced ecclesiology of Vatican II over Vatican I,

49

especially as formulated in the *Dogmatic Constitution on the Church*. As such, it also represents a step forward in the long road towards reunion: perhaps the Eastern Churches and the Anglican communion could one day accept again a petrine ministry that fostered and maintained and nurtured "communion between the communities, the local Churches" exercised in a true spirit of collegiality, the bishop of Rome acting in collaboration, in communication with all the bishops of the Church throughout the world.

In considering Church life since the Reformation, the Council begins by saying that it will not try, in the decree, to describe and define all these Churches and ecclesial communities. In other words, the Council refused to pronounce itself on the situation in the West. This might appear negative, but in fact it is clear, with hindsight, that it was a prophetic blessing in disguise, and therefore once again, a step forward. This position left the door open to future evolution of theological thinking, ecclesiological in particular. Even if the Council had refused to say which ecclesial realities in the West are "Churches" in the same sense as the decree spoke just before of the "Eastern Churches" or the "Churches of the East," at least it does affirm that there are some. Three times in four short paragraphs in the section entitled "The Separated Churches and Ecclesial Communities in the West," the decree repeats the phrase "Churches and ecclesial communities":

> The Churches and ecclesial communities which were separated from the Apostolic See of Rome...differ considerably not only from us, but also among themselves...Between these Churches and ecclesial communities...and the Catholic Church...there are very weighty differences (19).

That these references are rather negative—they refer to divisions and differences of these ecclesial realities in relation to the Catholic Church—only increases the significance that the text did in fact speak of Churches in the West. In 1964, the Council did not want to specify these Churches, with one exception: in the official report of the *modi* of the Council Fathers—but not in the text of the decree itself—the Old Catholic Churches are recognized as true local Churches because they have valid bishops and therefore valid sacraments. This is the same, actually the unique, criterion used in the decree to define where the Church truly exists in a given time and place. It was given a positive expression in the section on the Eastern Churches:

> These Churches, although separated from us, yet possess true sacraments, above all—by apostolic succession—the priesthood and the Eucharist (15).

In this section on the Western communities, it is given a negative expression, explaining why in some cases the Church does not exist sufficiently to be named as such:

> The ecclesial communities separated from us...have not preserved the proper reality of the Eucharistic mystery in its fullness, especially because of the absence of the sacrament of Orders (22).

It is important to note that, in the above passage, the decree does not use the phrase "the Churches and ecclesial communities" at the beginning of the section. What is the Council trying to say? Is it not this: if there are ecclesial realities in the West that possess the sacrament of Orders—through valid bishops in the apostolic succession—then they can legitimately be named local Churches; they are truly the Church in a given time and place.

A most conservative interpretation of the decree in its use of "Churches" in the West would say it could be speaking only of the Old Catholic Churches, and even then it did not want to mention them by name. One argument against such a narrow interpretation is that the decree does refer to one of the Western ecclesial bodies by name, even if it does not call it a Church in the same sentence:

> Still other divisions arose in the West...As a result, many communions...were separated from the Roman See. Among those in which Catholic traditions and institutions in part continue to exist, the Anglican communion occupies a special place (13).

With this thrice-used phrase, "the Churches and ecclesial communities," in the section on the Church in the West, and the above reference to the Anglican communion, a wider interpretation of the decree on this point is certainly possible and legitimate. It was a truly prophetic and hopeful stance that the Council adopted. It gave the Catholic Church itself the possibility of re-evaluating certain historical judgments it had made in the past on the separated communions of the West. It also left the door open to a theological justification for an eventual mutual recognition and reconciliation of ordained ministries between at least some of these communions and the Catholic Church. The Catholic Church, even in the West, could think of itself and those separated from it more in terms of estranged sisters trying to come together again and be reconciled, than of an authoritarian mother dictating the terms of eventual reunion ("return") to rebellious, recalcitrant daughters. In the years after the Council, this hopeful and helpful insight was to have a very beneficial influence on the theological accords on doctrinal questions in several national and international dialogues of the Roman Catholic Church with the Anglican, Lutheran, Orthodox and Reformed

Churches. Perhaps the most beautiful expression of it was made by Pope Paul VI six years after the Council:

> There will be no seeking to lessen the legitimate prestige and the worthy partrimony of piety and usage proper to the Anglican Church when the Roman Catholic Church—this humble "Servant of the servants of God"—is able to embrace her ever beloved Sister in the one authentic communion of the family of Christ.[3]

CONCLUSION

How has the whole Church received this decree and applied it in the Church's daily and weekly (especially the Lord's Day) ecclesial life? This is a very difficult question to answer for several reasons: the situations of the Churches in myriad places throughout the world are so different, so variable, that it is virtually impossible to generalize; any response to the question risks being influenced by subjective elements (in ecumenism more than other areas of ecclesial life the choice of "seeing the glass half full or half empty" is unavoidable); and any facts are often simply not known—numerous ecumenical experiences happen, some enduringly, on a very local level and are never known about in the Church at large.

In spite of these difficulties, it is possible to hazard a partial response. Considered alone, the *Decree on Ecumenism* has not been received by the Church any more than the whole body of teaching of the Second Vatican Council has been. I agree with many theologians that the Council has nowhere been sufficiently received by the Church. Conversely, we would affirm that some teachings of the Council have been received by the Church to a considerably greater degree, even if still insufficient, than the teaching on ecumenism. In the 1980's, most Roman Catholics have partially renewed their understandings of the Church (including biblical images), of a certain primacy of the Word of God in their daily lives, and of the eucharistic liturgy and their personal role in it. They do not seem to have even the same (still insufficient) understanding of their personal responsibility for fostering greater Christian unity.

This study ends with a few observations more directly related to the three themes that comprise the essential teaching of the *Decree on Ecumenism*. The first theme is the role of the Holy Spirit. In the past twenty years the charismatic renewal movement has flourished among many Christians of different Churches, including the Catholic Church. This movement has been a positive experience on the level of non-cultic, non-liturgical prayer of many Christians, often across denominational lines, prayer in a common searching for a return to the essentials of baptismal life. Consciously or unconsciously, it has surely fostered Christian unity. The real danger, however, is that the experience of the role of the Holy Spirit may become something parallel to our experience of the institutional Church.

Concerning the second theme, the role of every member of the Church in working for Christian unity, some truly wonderful things have happened. Who would have thought twenty years ago that, in the early 1980's, the Churches would have concluded theological discussion that resulted in accords—bilateral or multilateral—on the essential doctrinal questions of justification, baptism, Eucharist, ministries, ordination, authority in the Church? This happened to such an extent that some Churches are almost embarrassed because they persisted in preserving their individual entities despite this doctrinal convergence presented to them for their acceptance.

Few foresaw in 1964 that there would emerge an almost immediate, constant and growing collaboration between the Churches in scores of ecumenical "coalitions" or "task forces" around the world on practical, pastoral or social justice issues. But while in some parts of the world, many ecumenical officers or commissions, and councils of Churches were established and even flourish, in other places virtually nothing ecumenical has happened among Christians. In any case, the major failure in this area, the role of every Church member working for Christian unity, has been the tendency to confine this responsibility to experts—ecumenical officers, ecumenical commissions, ecumenical theologians. For most parish pastors, for many bishops, and for the mass of the Catholic faithful, the work of Christian unity is simply not a priority. This is one of the reasons why much ecumenical prayer and other works of the early years have fallen into a routine or have even completely disappeared.

Concerning the third theme, the idea and experience of the Church, the reality in which the Spirit brings every baptized Christian, one undeniable benefit has been the reduction of antagonism, polemics, mutual ignorance and proselytising among Christians and among the Churches. Admittedly this has not happened between all kinds of Christians nor everywhere around the world, but it is clear that this has been a general improvement. As well, most Roman Catholics are now at least vaguely aware of the ecclesial reality lived by their separated brethren. In other words, they realize that the Church exists beyond the visible boundaries of the Roman Catholic Church. Unfortunately, one must note the absence of "covenanting" between the Churches, at all levels —parish, diocese, regional, national and international. The idea of "sister Churches" that has emerged from the dialogue over the past twenty years is truly beautiful and hopeful. This idea, however, needs to be put into practice, otherwise it will disappear.

Whatever has happened ecumenically in the last twenty years has taken place during the most massive exodus of baptized Christians from

Church membership and participation that Christianity has experienced in its history. How easily the Churches forget or ignore this fact. Is there a link between this exodus, and the Churches' resistance, reluctance or even open refusal to make the unity of all Christians, the reconciliation and reunion of all the Churches, their first task?

Jesus Christ prayed for the unity of his disciples "in order that the world may believe that You, Father, have sent me…that [my disciples] be one as we are one…that the world know that You have sent me and that I have loved them as You have loved me" (Jn 17:21–23). The divisions of Christ's disciples must not prevent our non-Christian brethren from ever hearing and hoping in the Good News of the one, true, creating, loving, liberating God, and his "Sent One," Jesus the Christ.

Notes

1.   It is interesting to note that in Rublev's icon of the Trinity in the perfect circle and triangle formed by the three figures, only one element points outside that circle/triangle towards the earth, the world—the hand, the finger of the Holy Spirit.

2.   Pope Paul VI, *Acta Apostolicae Sedis*, 62 (1970), 754.

Decree on Priestly Formation

Optatam Totius

JOSEPH SCHNER

THE DOCUMENT

On October 28, 1965, the Council Fathers of Vatican II promulgated the *Decree on Priestly Formation, Optatam Totius*. Although it is a brief document, its contents range from the promotion of vocations (chap. 2), through programming for seminaries (chaps. 2 to 6), to a brief mention of on-going priestly formation (chap. 7).

On December 7 of the same year, a second decree, *Presbyterorum Ordinis*, on the ministry and life of priests, detailed the goal of formation.[1] The ordained is at the same time one with the ministry of Christ and one with those he serves as brothers and sisters (chap. 1). In ministry, he is to proclaim the Word of God and administer the sacraments within the Christian community and in union with other ordained ministers (chap. 2). Such ministry requires a personal life of holiness, obedience, celibacy, and voluntary poverty (chap. 3).

The formation decree, the topic of this essay, began as two documents, *De Vocationibus* and *De Sacrorum Alumnis*, and was presented as such in January 1962 to the preparatory Central Commission of the Council by the preparatory Seminary Commission. The commission asked that the two documents be amalgamated.[2] Despite a complex history, the final document is comparatively short, consisting of only twenty-two articles.[3] The preface links the decree with the traditions of the past and with the renewal of the Council. Chapter 1 makes the implementation of the decree the responsibility of the Episcopal Conference and the religious ordinary. Chapter 2 deals with the fostering and discernment of priestly vocations.

Chapter 3 begins the discussion of priestly formation. The goal of such formation is the training of true shepherds for the ministry of the

Word, of the Eucharist, and of pastoral service. This training should be carried out by directors with high qualifications, in regional or national seminaries that encourage the personal development of the individual within community. There should be an on-going evaluation of this formation.

Chapter 4 discusses the necessary spiritual formation of the individual into the Mystery of Christ. This formation should be aided by sound spiritual direction complemented by a knowledge of developmental psychology. The decree recommends an intensive, initial period that teaches the fundamentals of prayer and the spiritual and liturgical life, as well as the history, of Christian spirituality.

In chapter 5, the decree turns to a focal point—the revision of ecclesiastical studies. Both academic and pastoral courses should be oriented towards priestly ministry. The Mystery of Christ and the history of salvation must be central in these studies, which also consider the realities of the contemporary world. They should be undertaken with awareness of current ecumenical efforts.

Chapter 6 completes this revision of studies by insisting on pastoral training as an integral part of formation through the use of modern methods and with the provision of practical experience.

The final chapter reminds Episcopal Conferences that priestly formation is an on-going process and provisions must be made for continuing studies for all priests.

COMPLEMENTARY DOCUMENTS

This initial document has generated a number of subsidiary documents that specify its contents and their implementation. Two levels of sources exist: the Roman Curial level, and the national or religious congregation level. There are also two strategies of implementation coming from these sources: general "plans" and specific "programs."

In 1970, at the request of the First Synod of Bishops, the Congregation for Catholic Education published a first set of guidelines, *The Basic Plan for Priestly Formation*. Several circular letters and documents followed: *The Teaching of Philosophy in Seminaries* (1972), *Guidelines for Formation for Priestly Celibacy* (1974), *Theological Formation of Future Priests* (1976), *Instruction on Liturgical Formation in Seminaries* (1979), and "Circular Letter Concerning Some of the More Urgent Aspects of Spiritual Formation in Seminaries" (1980). Finally, in 1983, the new Code of Canon Law devoted thirty-two canons (nos. 232 to 264) to a summary of directives from these documents. Paralleling these documents were national and religious ones: in Canada, *The Program of Priestly Formation* (1981), in the United States, *The Program of Priestly Formation* (1968, 1976 and 1981), and in the

Society of Jesus, *General Norms for Jesuit Studies* (1980), *Order of Studies of Upper Canada Province* (1982), and *Regional Order of Studies for the American Assistancy* (1983).

Each document returns to and explicitates *Optatam Totius*. In its introduction, the *Basic Plan* takes up a point that was covered in one sentence in the decree: "Major seminaries are necessary for priestly formation." The *Basic Plan* describes as primary the role of the seminary as a community and way of life rather than as an institution. The *Basic Plan*, however, does emphasize some "institutional" aspects of the seminary: professors, superiors, and courses of study. It also deals with spiritual formation and pastoral ministry, both as essential components of seminary life. In reference to these, it gives special attention to training towards a celibate life.[4] During the next decade, the Congregation for Catholic Education issued five documents that addressed specific aspects of the *Basic Plan*. In 1972, in relation to philosophical formation, it published *The Teaching of Philosophy in Seminaries* (chap. 11 of the *Basic Plan*). This document defended the need for philosophical studies as formative of the type of thinking that is competent to deal with theological problems, and as a means for real dialogue with non-believers.

In 1974, the Congregation published a document entitled *Guidelines for Formation for Priestly Celibacy* (chap. 8). This document began with a theological explanation of the meaning of celibacy in the ordained life, and outlined three goals of seminary training in light of this: human, Christian, and priestly maturity. Practical guidelines followed to help in fostering celibacy in seminary life.

In 1976, the Congregation issued *The Theological Formation of Future Priests* (chap. 12). It is parallel to the document on philosophy. In a changing world of technology and materialism, theology must be taught so as to be comprehensible to twentieth-century people who are more familiar with the intricacies of the laser, for example, than the mysteries of a transcendent God. At the same time, the traditions of Christianity must be respected and preserved. As prescribed by the documents of Vatican II, theology must be studied in the context of pluralism and ecumenism.

Two documents appeared in 1980, *Instruction on Liturgical Formation in Seminaries* (chaps. 8 and 12), and a circular letter "Concerning Some of the More Urgent Aspects of Spiritual Formation in Seminaries" (chap. 8). The first treated both the theoretical and practical aspects of liturgical formation, and described the liturgical topics to be discussed in seminary courses: the nature of the liturgy, including its instructive and pastoral dimensions, and its history; the Mass; and the sacraments. The second elaborated on the *Basic Plan* in four fundamental areas: prayer, Eucharist, penance, and Marian devotion.

All of these documents then had to be applied in the local Churches. This was done through a second set of documents originating from the National Conferences of Bishops and from the Congregations of Religious. For example, the United States Conference of Bishops published three editions of *The Program of Priestly Formation*. The third edition was prepared jointly with the Conference of Congregations of Religious Men in the United States. It dealt with the details of training at three levels—seminary, college, and high school—and set forth specific guidelines for each.

After a number of delays, the Canadian Conference of Bishops published its *Program of Priestly Formation* in 1981. This *Program* was more general than the American and left many details to the statutes of the six formation centres in Canada, for example, the specific plan of philosophical courses required before theology, and the theology curriculum itself.

A comparable flow of documents followed the Vatican document on religious congregations like the Society of Jesus. In 1968, the interim *General Norms for Studies* was promulgated by Pedro Arrupe, to be followed in 1980 with the definitive *General Norms*. Assistancies or provinces implemented these at the local level through Orders of Studies, for example, the Upper Canada Province in 1982, and the American Assistancy in 1983.

THE RESULTS

One might justly wonder about the results of this barrage of documents. Because of the low number of seminarians today, it is a temptation to suggest, with hindsight, that the Council ought to have looked more closely at the question of vocation to the ordained ministry, rather than just at formation. Although there is a detailed plan for formation, today there are few men to be trained by this plan. It was as if the Council had little doubt that vocations would continue to increase (as in fact they did until the mid-1960's). But such questions as celibacy, hierarchical authority, and the ordination of women—within cultures that emphasize sexual expression, personal liberty and a growing emancipation of women's roles in society—seem to discourage (or forbid, in the case of women) candidates from applying or persevering. Such fundamental questions still need a response from the Roman Church, a need not addressed by *Optatam Totius* or succeeding documents.

In general, however, during the nearly twenty years since the promulgation of *Optatam Totius*, formation itself has indeed changed in some of its aspects. In 1967, Robert Johann, then a Jesuit professor of philosophy at Fordham University in New York, saw two tasks for seminary reformation: "the effort...to bring the seminaries more closely in line with the standards and practices of American colleges and universities"; and in conjunction with this academic move, the necessity of "a way of achieving genuine communal solidarity without subordinating persons to structures, and a way of achieving a genuine personalism...without the dissolution of community."[5] Without this solidarity, he forecast the alternative of individualistic humanism. What Johann was aiming at was a realistic communal life for a priest, one of social and affective support in the context of faith and vocation, but which would not require conformity to some stereotypical pattern or image of ordained ministry and of community as the price for such support. The alternative to such a community is a personal isolation that threatens both vocation and faith.

The first of Johann's tasks, the adaptation of academic programs, has certainly been achieved in Canada. Economics and the demands of academic respectability helped this process by forcing the closing of small understaffed diocesan seminaries. In 1968, Elliott Allen, of the University of St. Michael's College, foresaw a new context for the study of theology in an ecumenical and professional/pastoral setting.[6] This prediction has come about in consortia like the Toronto and the Atlantic Schools of Theology, which provide resources for high academic standards and immerse students for the ministry in the experience of university scholarship and interdenominational co-operation. At the same time, they foster strong pastoral components in their basic master of divinity programs in conjunction with an active clinical pastoral education movement in Canada. In addition, with religious and lay master's and doctoral students in theological faculties, it is necessary to have upper level faculty and the accompanying library and research resources. Academic standards have also been bolstered by professional groups such as the Association of Theological Schools.

These academic and professional advances have taken place with the help of *Optatam Totius* and the decrees, especially *Lumen Gentium*, of Vatican II. Today, F.X. Sullivan sees that the situation "differs from that which prevailed two decades ago chiefly in two respects: the disappearance of the old neo-scholastic manuals and the institution of 'field education' for seminarians."[7] But addressing the latter, he questions this learning of "skills" in the seminary; seminaries suffer from the "neglect of fundamentals in favor of techniques." He favours more emphasis in the seminary on doctrinal tradition and moral theology. Field education should not dominate such teaching.

This criticism, if nothing else, is evidence of the academic changes that have taken place and the challenge of integrating doctrinal and pastoral theology that exists.

There is slower progress, however, in the area of that "genuine communal solidarity" and "genuine personalism" that Johann stressed as essential to the renovation of priestly formation. *Optatam Totius* (chap. 4) does indeed speak of psychological maturity and the community life of candidates; this is developed by the *Basic Plan* (chap. 8), the *Guidelines for Formation for Priestly Celibacy*, the "Circular Letter Concerning Some of the More Urgent Aspects of Spiritual Formation in Seminaries," and the new Canon 244. But the issue of human and community development is approached more from the perspective of an ascetic theology—theological reasons for the need for obedience, sacrifice, silence, and devotion to the Blessed Virgin Mary—rather than from the perspective of the social sciences. For example, no mention is made of such helpful psychological theories as the stages of development described by Erikson, Kohlberg, or Fowler, and especially of the crucial stages of adolescence and young adulthood, identification, and intimacy.[8] Nor do there appear to be guidelines for the formation of that community which the documents take for granted.

The *Guidelines for Formation for Priestly Celibacy* is no more useful to the seminarian in its neglect of exactly these fundamental aspects of individual and social development. Its scholastic manner speaks of "habits of virtue," and places emotional drives "at the service of...reason":

> A well-integrated person knows how to make his reason rule his emotional nature, while the less adjusted a person is, the more his emotions will dominate his rational nature. Therefore, an educational program that aims to form a well-developed personality must above all help the students to acquire the ability to balance their emotions.[9]

It does not deal with questions of intimacy and sexual expression; reason and rationality are to reign supreme. This is more like the realm of Johann's subordination of persons to structures, in this instance the structure of psychological repression where emotional expression and affective intimacy are ignored as if non-existent. In fact, for "to balance" one ought to read "to repress." Regarding community, the *Guidelines* go on to speak of "a brotherhood and a union of love" that foster emotional and sexual integration.[10] But it appears the goal is one of a cool, rational community where persons are capable, no doubt, of social niceties but keep their emotional and sexual distance. It sheds no light on the human development underlying and needed for a healthy and realistic "union of love."

Matthias Neuman, a member of the faculty of St. Meinrad Seminary, Indiana, briefly analyzes the resulting ordained ministry and the actual community:

> How can one describe this prevalent socio-psychological judgment of priesthood that dominates the seminary ethos? That Catholic priests as a

group are somewhat effective personally, materially privileged, institutional power figures, but also lonely and frustrated men! They live a life filled with conflicts: celibacy, obedience to the bishop and Rome, strife with other priests, disputes with various lay groups, justice pressures, etc....The prevailing social interaction of many diocesan seminaries, being all-male, becomes highly competitive and continuously evaluative...One major problem which results from four years in this enclosed competitive environment is that an individual's personal goals frequently tend to shrink toward exclusively intra-institutional and egotistical ones...One sometimes has the impression of watching 24- to 25-year old men trying to prove to their all-male companions how macho they are.[11]

Through the theological schools, most Canadian seminaries have left an all-male society. I would, however, have to agree with Neuman's critique. After several years of involvement in priestly formation, I conclude that the psychological and social maturity of candidates for orders remains a serious problem, even in the consortia setting. Seminarians, like Neuman's "new conservatives," centre their ministry on individual, spiritual direction of personal prayer, on personal counselling, and on cultic ministry; there are activists of both left and right who substitute an ideology for interpersonal, intimate relationships, and deal with the faithful from the safety of their ideology.[12] For a few of these, the reality of the contemporary world intrudes with resulting trauma leading either to growth or to flight. At the same time, these men put heavy pressures on the seminary community. Responding to their need for psychological growth so that they can live humanly and effectively in community is a challenge to the post-conciliar Church, one that I do not believe is being faced.

It is this failure that writers are reporting in the popular North American Catholic press. For example, the *National Catholic Reporter* in February 1983 devoted its Forum to the topic "Seminarians as Endangered Species."[13] And yet, the American Seminary Visitation, ordered by John Paul II in 1981 reportedly at the request of some American bishops, and the investigation of St. Augustine's Seminary in Toronto by Bishop Marcel Gervais in 1984, seemed more concerned with the issues of orthodoxy, the presence of women as faculty members and spiritual directors in seminary programs, lay involvement in theological training, and conformity with the traditional stereotype of ordained ministers. Such investigations are symptomatic of an attempt to make seminary training a safe, authority-oriented and clerical preserve, where the tension of community and personal development can be safely monitored and contained, and the new priest helped to take on this stereotype.

The "signs of the times"—the social analysis that Vatican II so frequently reminds us of—suggest that in such a preserve lies the end of seminary life. It may be that only with the seminary's demise can the formation for ordained ministry start on a new path to academic, professional and ecumenical excellence, and also as *Optatam Totius* hoped for, psychologically and socially mature ministers.

Notes

1.   A.P. Flannery, ed., "Decree on the Ministry and Life of Priests," *The Documents of Vatican II* (New York: Pillar Books, 1975).
2.   Josef Neumer, "Decree on Priestly Formation," in *Commentary on the Documents of Vatican II*, ed. H. Vorgrimler, vol. 2 (New York: Herder, 1968), 371–404.b3.   A.P. Flannery, ed., "Decree on Priestly Formation," *The Documents of Vatican II* (New York: Pillar Books, 1975). For summary and commentary, see Peter M. Collins, "Vatican II's Decree on Priestly Formation: A Pedagogical Commentary I," *Clergy Review*, 67 (1982), 26.
4.   For a detailed commentary on the *Basic Plan*, see O. De Lettero, "Basic Scheme for Priestly Formation," *Clergy Monthly*, 34 (1970), 306–34.
5.   Robert O. Johann, "New Strategies in Catholic Seminary Training," *Union Seminary Quarterly Review*, 22 (1967), 349–55.
6.   Elliott B. Allen, "The Roman Catholic Seminary: Changing Perspectives in Theological Education," *Canadian Journal of Theology*, 14 (1968), 159–68.
7.   Francis X. Sullivan, "Preparing for Priestly Ministry in the 'Eighties'," *The Priest*, 37 (1981), 19–21.
8.   For a fuller discussion of these, see J.G. Schner, "The Escape from Intimacy," *The Pius Riffel Lecture* (Toronto: Regis College Press, 1984).
9.   "A Guide to Formation in Priestly Celibacy," *Origins*, 4, no. 4 (1974), 66–76.
10.   "Guide," par. 26.
11.   Matthias Neuman, "Assessing Priestly Formation Today," *The Priest*, 41 (Oct. 1981), 39–45.
12.   Matthias Neuman, "Seminaries and the New Conservatives," *America*, 137 (1977), 126–7.
13.   *National Catholic Reporter*, Feb. 25, 1983, 7–24.

Decree on the Appropriate Renewal of the Religious Life

Perfectae Caritatis

MARGARET BRENNAN

In 1967, one year after the close of the Council, Edward Schillebeeckx wrote the following:

> The "adaptation of the religious life" must be, first and foremost, a re-evangelizing of all its structures. The consequences of this conciliar maxim are more numerous than a superficial reading of it would seem to indicate. The text gives the church an inspiration whose charismatic consequences, I feel, cannot even be surmised at this moment. But eventually this "supreme rule" will break through, without any clashes, we trust, though some will well occur...

The twenty years since the Council have seen both the charismatic consequences of the re-evangelizing of religious life and the clashes. The promulgation of the new Code of Canon Law in 1983 and other documents coming from the Sacred Congregation for Religious in Rome have prescribed a delineation for the present and future shape of religious life, bringing an end to what was called a "period of experimentation." Yet that reflection on the experience of the past two decades has caused many religious women to be uneasy with prescriptive norms that are often regressive and appear to halt the very impetus initiated by the Vatican Council.

In this essay I will discuss the Vatican documents that gave both the mandate and the impetus for the renewal of religious life, trace the story of how these documents were understood and actualized in the lives of religious women, and describe some challenges and hopes for the future. I am restricting this to women religious simply because I do not have enough information to reflect on how the experience has touched orders of men. Furthermore, since this account depends upon my experience as a North American, it cannot be said to be normative for women religious of other cultures. Nevertheless, because the same Canon Law governed religious everywhere, there was great similarity in meeting the challenge of change, albeit in a variety of circumstances.

THE VATICAN DOCUMENTS THAT GAVE THE MANDATE AND IMPETUS FOR RENEWAL

Two documents of Vatican II refer specifically to the renewal of religious life: the *Dogmatic Constitution on the Church, Lumen Gentium* (chapter 6), and the *Decree on the Appropriate Renewal of the Religious Life, Perfectae Caritatis*. The principles laid down in these two documents found a context in three other documents: the *Pastoral Constitution on the Church in the Modern World*, the *Decree on the Church's Missionary Activity*, and the *Declaration on Religious Freedom*. It is the understanding of this contextuality that has often been the source of the tension that continues between many religious congregations and the Sacred Congregation for Religious, over the appropriate renewal of religious life and the re-evangelizing of its structures.

A look at how these documents were constructed gives some insight into the character of their final form. *Commentaries on the Documents* of Vatican II, published by Herder and Herder in 1967, provides that information in detail. Here I will rely on the commentaries written by Friedrich Wulf on *Lumen Gentium* and *Perfectae Caritatis*.

Perhaps that most essential change in a renewed understanding of religious life is found in chapters 5 and 6 of *Lumen Gentium*. These chapters, which consider the call of the whole Church to holiness, should be read as a whole. Their construction involved long and sometimes heated debates. Some bishops favoured one chapter within which religious life would be seen in the total context of the universal call to holiness. Others, fearing such inclusion would diminish or belittle the religious state, pressed for a special chapter that would highlight and recognize the particular gift that religious life brings to the Church's life of holiness. In the end, the second position prevailed; the signs of compromise make the chapters less clear and strong than the others in the documents. Nevertheless, in them can be found the theological basis for an understanding of religious life that, in my opinion, has moved significantly away from what existed before.

In *Lumen Gentium*, the Church defines itself as the People of God who are all equally called to holiness and perfection. The clerical and religious states are not to be thought of as higher or better than that of the laity, who are "in their own way made sharers in the priestly, prophetic, and kingly functions of Christ" (31). The longstanding and traditional terminology describing religious life as a state of perfection is no longer used. Those who profess the evangelical counsels of poverty, chastity and obedience by special vow or sacred bond in distinct forms of community life approved by the Church should not be considered as entering an intermediate state between clerical and lay, but rather a way of life open to both (43). Religious life is a gift of the Holy Spirit to the Church, to assist it in carrying out its life and mission. It does not belong to the hierarchical structure of the Church, but finds its place in respect to its charismatic life and holiness (44).

The concluding articles of chapter 6 summarize this new understanding. Through religious life, the Church wishes to give an increasingly clearer revelation of Christ in his saving mission through his obedience to the Father who sent him. Such a life is genuinely human; those who enter into it are not to be seen and should not consider themselves as strangers to other men and women or useless citizens of the earthly city (44).

A pastoral understanding of these statements and their pastoral implementation in life and mission have radicalized the understanding of religious life and founded a new conception. I will refer to the implications later.

The *Decree of the Appropriate Renewal of Religious Life* does not add new insights to chapter 6 of *Lumen Gentium*, but instead spells out more clearly the pastoral and theological implications within such a renewed understanding.

The decree passed through four revisions. The final draft was almost unanimously accepted on October 28, 1965.

The work of the commissions that prepared it passed through the important shift in the Council itself, between the second and third sessions, when the Council's pastoral orientation was further strengthened and articulated.

The bishops' interest in this decree was somewhat mixed, at times even apathetic, perhaps because the debate on chapters 5 and 6 of *Lumen Gentium* seemed to be the basic dogmatic discussion about the role of religious in the life and mission of the Church. They seemed anxious to move on.

The heated discussions over the revisions of the decree on religious renewal were often between those bishops who were themselves members of religious orders or congregations and were struggling to safeguard the forms and traditions of religious life.

The first draft drawn up by the Preparatory Commission reflected a lack of unity and little outside consultation, and was juridical in tone. In 1962, the formation of a Commission for Religious Orders under the direction of Archbishop P. Philippe, O.P., was entrusted with continuing the revision. The second, third and fourth drafts, which took the better part of the next two years (1962–64), had to deal with the diversity of views about the nature of religious life and how to accommodate the renewal. It was not a easy task. The commission had been instructed to prepare a very brief schema. It was to exclude all juridical elements, to be more pastoral in accord with the direction of the Council, and to provide simple and clear guidelines for renewal. Many bishops believed (as was previously mentioned) that *Lumen Gentium* had already dealt with the dogmatic aspects.

Somewhat surprisingly, the fourth draft, presented in September 1964, was hotly debated. Two sharply opposing views surfaced among the bishops. Some pressed for a clear exposition and clear regulations to safeguard the essentials and the institutions of religious life. Another group, in sharp disagreement, stressed the need for a courageous attack on the weaknesses in religious life that prevented it from being an influential force in the Church and society. They pointed to its inadequately based spirituality, one-sided attitude to superiors, out-of-date forms, lack of missionary spirit, and inadequate education for its members.

The fifth and final draft withdrew from attempting a short schema with only the essential guidelines and prepared instead a version that tried to incorporate the numerous, diverse, and contradictory messages received from the bishops. This text bears the marks of the compromises that had to be made. For example, the first paragraph in article 5 reflects the dispute about the nature of the evangelical counsels, to whom they are addressed, and whether they constitute a higher, better way for religious:

> The members of each community should recall above everything else that by their profession of the evangelical counsels they have given answer to a divine call to live for God alone not only by dying to sin (cf. Rom 6:11) but also by renouncing the world. They have handed over their entire lives to God's service in an act of special consecration and which provides an ampler manifestation of it.

In his commentary on the decree, Wulf suggests the following questions: Do religious, as the article indicates, renounce the world by the profession of the evangelical counsels? Does one who follows the counsels literally live for God alone? How does the decree reflect the tone of the *Pastoral Constitution on the Church in the Modern World*, which takes exception to this view? And what does this say of the laity who have also been called in their own way to follow the counsels?

In spite of its shortcomings, the decree did succeed in pointing out the principles that underlie the direction the renewal of religious life should take. The differing ecclesiologies at work within its articulation have, however, kept opposing views alive in today's understanding of religious life.

Because the decree did not intend to deal with the details of accommodating the renewal, Pope Paul VI published the apostolic letter

Ecclesiae Sanctae in August 1966. This provided guidelines for experimentation. It mandated all religious congregations to invoke special chapters within the next three years to implement the renewal called for by the Council. A post-conciliar commission made up of members of the original commission, assisted by fifteen consultants, was empowered to draw up the general norms.

The renewal chapters invited the religious to a serious study of the Council documents, together with sustained and intense reflection on the experience of religious life. No other group of persons in the Church took more seriously the mandate of the Council, and having courageously implemented its principles, no other group has experienced its effects more dramatically. It is this journey and experience that I now examine.

UNDERSTANDING AND CARRYING OUT THE DOCUMENTS IN THE LIVES OF NORTH AMERICAN RELIGIOUS

Apostolic religious life for women on the eve of the Council was a hierarchically structured, semi-monastic form of life. The Code of 1917 had prescribed numerous regulations about religious governance, the profession and practice of the vows, the formation of novices, and the exercise of the apostolate. These were reflected in rules of life that governed every moment of the day. Elements of cloister and separation from the world curtailed contact with "seculars," which was limited to the hours dedicated to the exercise of the apostolate and occasional visits from family. The works of religious were basically institutional and carried out in most cases under the mandate of the local bishop. The apostolic impetus and charisms that had given birth to religious congregation were, as a result, often lost under prescriptions that hindered rather than enhanced the purposes for which they were founded.

Vatican II interrupted this hierarchically ordered way of life with a call to self-understanding and self-determination. In the last twenty years this has resulted in a new shift, with consequences, to borrow the phrase of Schillebeeckx, that "cannot even be surmised at this moment."

Religious women in North America seemed better prepared than most others for the meaning of the renewal. In the 1950's, the Sister-Formation Movement had already led many congregations in the teaching and healing apostolates to recognize the need for a more adequate formation and academic education of novices and junior professed to exercise their ministries. Many houses of formation were erected. And in colleges of their own, on secular campuses or Catholic universities, young women pursued academic degrees that professionally prepared them to administer hospitals and work in educational institutions. The same attention was given to spiritual and human formation. In many cases, this movement led to conflict as the years of preparation caused personnel shortages and brought in lay people who began to work side by side with religious. Whereas before the education of religious had been spread over seventeen or eighteen summers, religious were now fully prepared and equal to their lay colleagues as they began their apostolic life. A decade of such formation formed fertile minds and shaped the ability to make critical judgments. As a result, the seed of renewal was able to fall on good ground in many communities.

But the years of the late sixties and early seventies were also ones of turmoil for religious congregations and the hierarchy. It was both challenging and confusing to make into one's own the new concepts initiated by the Council. Diverse views of renewal based on the differing ecclesiologies in the documents of Vatican II brought pain and internal division among the members of communities and between communities themselves. In the United States, this was epitomized in the tension between religious superiors. In North America, in opposition to the more liberal views of the officially established Leadership Conference of Women Religious (formerly the Conference of Major Superiors of Women), a significant number of superiors general formed a common conference, the Consortium Perfectae Caritatis. Many bishops were divided in their allegiance to one group or another and in time, the Sacred Congregation of Religious joined the controversy as it tried to bring them together.

On the positive side, the study of other Vatican documents, particularly the *Pastoral Constitution on the Church in the Modern World* and the *Decree on the Church's Missionary Activity*, with their calls to be in the world and to serve the poor and the marginalized, led many religious into ministries among the elderly, prisoners, the Black community, Native peoples, and the oppressed in Latin America, and to live religious life among the people they served. Many left their spacious convents to live in simple neighbourhood dwellings. Religious habits gave way to secular dress, and enclosed monastic lives with structured prayer forms changed to new forms of prayer and community that gave life to the faith-sharing of religious. Heightened social consciousness motivated religious communities and individuals to challenge unjust political and economic structures at home and abroad, while anti-war and pacifist movements engaged a significant number in civil disobedience.

For many bishops, the move of religious women into diverse non-institutional ministries loosened the ties between the religious and the hierarchy in the ordering of apostolic works. These changes to a more non-structured religious way of life brought tension and misunderstanding, which in some cases reached crisis proportion, as in the case of the

California Immaculate Heart of Mary Sisters who were pressured into non-canonical status.

In Rome, the Sacred Congregation of Religious reacted with alarm and concern. And in North America, the religious communities tried, with difficulty, to reflect their experience and have it understood. In some instances, apostolic visitations were conducted in response to the pleas of more traditionally oriented groups of sisters in their communities. This sometimes caused divisions that hardened into irrevocable splits.

The situation was more volatile in the United States than in Canada, especially in the 1960's. During that decade, the optimism of the 1950's gave way to an awareness of oppression under the facade of the post-war economic boom. As religious women were examining their own role in the Church and society, they discovered that they would take their place in a world of struggle and turmoil. It was a world where race riots broke out in many United States cities. The United States involvement in Vietnam caused disillusionment and a loss of prestige, reflected in student unrest on many university campuses. And the assassinations of John and Robert Kennedy, Malcolm X and Martin Luther King Jr. added the lack of hope and sense of meaninglessness. But then there had also been the civil right movement, with the significant march in Selma under the leadership of Martin Luther King Jr., which many religious joined. The influence of Philip and Dan Berrigan, and the writings of Thomas Merton and John Howard Griffin radicalized the thinking of religious and made them conscious of the urgency of concerted action in the organization of peace movements and anti-war protests.

Canada had similar movements but on a lesser scale. Its cultural unrest could be seen in the regional differences brought about by economic inequity, in student demonstrations, in the movements of Native peoples for greater equality and justice on reserves and in the cities, in the growing power of the anti-war movement, and in concern for the plight of many immigrant peoples. Today religious women in Canada are active in all of these areas.

CHALLENGES AND HOPES FOR THE FUTURE

The proceedings of the Leadership Conference of Women Religious and of the Canadian Religious Conference over the past fifteen years show an understanding of the life and mission of religious that has gone beyond the initial thrust of Vatican II. In many cases, the decrees have been reinterpreted in the light of their experience.

Religious are now more aware that their lives are not determined by their position in a hierarchically structured Church as was clearly stated in *Lumen Gentium* (43, 44), but rather by the demands of their particular mission and call to holiness. The same *Dogmatic Constitution on the Church* reminds religious that "the spiritual life...should be devoted to the welfare of the whole Church. Thence arises their duty of working to implant and strengthen the Kingdom of Christ in souls and to extend the Kingdom in every land" (44). Reinterpreting their lives in terms of the Church *in* mission, they find that their understanding of ministry, their pursuit of holiness, their living of the vows and community life, must be grounded in this realization. Their experiences of the lessons in the *Pastoral Constitution on the Church in the Modern World*, the *Decree on the Church's Missionary Activity*, and the *Declaration on Religious Freedom* have inspired them to overcome the sacred/secular dichotomy and have led them to a diversification of ministries beyond the confines of institutional and Church apostolates. The missionary character of the Church is a question of human liberation, leading religious into ministries of advocacy for the poor, social work in government agencies, political lobbying for economic justice, and work with Christians and non-Christians alike for nuclear disarmament and the promotion of peace.

The pursuit of holiness, that is, the profession of poverty, celibacy and obedience, has been made more communal. Union with God, to be enjoyed in ultimate beatitude, finds its realization now in an understanding of religious life that draws its inspiration from incarnation and recognizes, in the words of Segundo Galilea, that "true prayer is the supreme act of abnegation and forgetfulness of self in order to encounter Christ and his demands in others."

The relationship between religious and the world they seek to serve had inevitably caused tension between experience and law which too often have little in common with their lives and even less with the Gospel. This tension and the concern religious women feel about the restrictive legislation governing their lives have not been resolved entirely by the new and "more enlightened" codification of Canon Law. In too many instances, its requirements no longer reflect their experience. Moreover, a whole generation of young religious women has been formed according to the mandate of Vatican II and a new understanding of religious life. The prescriptions required by many aspects of the Code and other curial requirements, such as those of the *Essential Elements in the Church's Teaching on Religious Life as Applied to Institutes Dedicated to the Works of the Apostolate*, promulgated by the Sacred Congregation for Religious in 1983, reverse the only experience of religious life they have lived and committed themselves to.

The past twenty years have shown that religious have only begun to realize what is essential to their lives. The attempts to codify the changes in their lives at this time are in danger of freezing what is but a moment within a long evaluation of North American religious women. This evaluation, begun by the Church, welcomed and urged forward by our society, is, I hope, inspired by the Gospel of Jesus Christ. Religious have, in a sense, "left their nets" as did the apostles—and they are earnestly attempting to follow the Lord. To be stopped half-way by continued legislation from Rome would be to be spared the Cross perhaps, but also never to share in the resurrection.

The last twenty years have also witnessed the rise of the women's movement in society, and the sharpening lines of a feminist theology in the Churches. Women religious, whose lives and ministries are dedicated to the mission of the Church, are increasingly aware that a full participation in its ministries and a full recognition of their equality are lacking.

The Vatican documents refer to women specifically on only five occasions—once in the *Decree on the Apostolate of the Laity* and four times in the *Pastoral Constitution on the Church in the Modern World*. The decree on the laity notes that "because women have a more active role in society they should participate more widely in the various fields of the Church's apostolate" (9). The other passages, all found in the *Pastoral Constitution on the Church in the Modern World*, are less encouraging and reflect an understanding of women based on specific "role" or "nature." These documents state that it "is appropriate that they [women] should be able to assume their full proper role in accordance with their own nature" (60); that women's domestic role "must be safely preserved, though the legitimate social progress of women should not be underrated on that account" (52); that a woman's right be safeguarded "to choose a husband, to embrace a state of life, or to acquire an education or cultural benefits equal to those recognized for men" (29); that "when they have not yet won it, women claim for themselves an equality with men before the law and in fact" (9).

The pastoral questions emerging from the ministerial experience of apostolic religious women have been made challengingly clear in the pressing need to consider changes of law and to search for new theological formulations that allow these women to serve the sacramental needs of Christians who call them to this exercise. For some women, their exclusion from orders by Church law is a statement of the inferiority of women Christians as Christians. To say, they argue, that any Christian is incapable *by nature* of receiving all of the sacraments, incapable *by nature* of full participation in the mystery of Christ, prophet, priest, king, is to say that there are two grades of Christians: complete and partial ones, first class and second class, superior and inferior, integral and defective. Moreover, they believe that the right and duty to determine and to discern whether a given vocation should be recognized by the community is not the right to place a priori limits on what the Spirit can call a person to, or when the Spirit may call.

But even more significant are the pastoral effects and the hindering of the Church's mission so urgently promoted by the Vatican documents.

71

Whole communities in the Church, in both developed and Third World countries, are being denied full sacramental life because of the shortage of ordained ministers. Apart from the question of equality of persons, such a grave situation must itself call forth a serious examination of the Church's teachings on ordination. Many women ministers are being seriously hampered in their apostolic activity because they cannot fully administer certain sacraments of which they are the natural and obvious ministers, for example, counsellors in prisons, and chaplains in hospitals.

More serious still is the situation in Third World countries where women are virtually the pastors for thousands of people without a priest except perhaps three or four times a year. What are we to answer to the prevalence of non-ordained ministers in many communities that are accustoming themselves and the nourishment of their faith to para-liturgies, deprived of the very heart of the Christian faith—a participation in the Eucharistic celebration of Jesus' saving death resurrection?

The Christian vision stressed in *Lumen Gentium* that "there is in Christ and in the Church no inequality on the basis of race, nationality, social conditions, or sex because there is in the words of Paul, 'neither Jew nor Greek, neither slave nor free, neither male nor female'" has never been realized by the Church. Though the Church and theology have maintained the equality of all Christians with respect to salvation, charity and grace, it has not done so with respect to ecclesial presence, leadership, and institutions.

As they reflect twenty years later on the meaning of who they are in the Church, women religious who return once again to the sources of Christian life for their renewal and ministry struggle with these questions.

Notes

1. Canadian Religious Conference, *Religious Life Renewed...Formation Reviewed (Donum Dei Series*, no. 28, 1983).
2. Galilea Segundo, "Liberation as an Encounter with Politics and Contemplation," *Concilium*, vol. 96 (New York: Herder and Herder, 1974).
3. Leadership Conference of Women Religious of the U.S.A., *Starting Points: Six Essays Based on the Experience of U.S. Religious Women* (Washington, D.C., 1980).
4. Edward Schillebeeckx, *Vatican II: The Real Achievement* (New York: Sheed and Ward, 1967).
5. H. Vorgrimler, ed., *Commentary on the Documents of Vatican II* (New York: Herder and Herder) vol. 1 (1967), vol. 2 (1968).

Decree on the Apostolate of the Laity

Apostolicam Actuositatem

ISIDORE GORSKI

On the eve of the Vatican II, it was customary to speak to the "emerging laity." After the Council had ended, however, many commentators thought that the laity still had not emerged; they thought that as the first Vatican Council was that of the papacy, so the second Council was really that of the episcopacy. Other commentators, however, disagreed and saw Vatican II above all as the Council of the laity.

I concur with the latter opinion, for the Council did give the laity an important place in its teaching. In a number of its documents, Vatican II highlighted a role for the laity in the apostolate of the Church.

If the Council had stopped there, one might wonder whether the assembly of bishops had been interested in the laity only for their usefulness. But the Council went further. In two of its documents, *Lumen Gentium* and *Apostolicam Actuositatem*, the Council spoke of the laity in a more internal way, that is, as to their relations with other groups in the Church itself. If it is true that the laity have really emerged, that they are playing their rightful role in the Church, this is not because of pastoral encouragement and organizational measures. The flowering of the laity has come about because of the theological self-understanding of the Church in Vatican II.

It is appropriate here to give an overview of the attitude of the Church toward the laity prior to the convocation of the ecumenical assembly in 1962. During the period of the New Testament, the Church was viewed primarily as a fellowship, a community that was contrasted with the world by its special relationship to God through Jesus Christ. The members of this fellowship were singled out from the world and formed into a special people by the call that went forth in Christ. The New Testament notes differences among this people, according to charisms and authority; nevertheless, it stresses the special gifts of the various people that serve to build up the community. There is no explicit distinction between officers and subjects, between clergy and laity.

In the post New Testament period up to the beginning of the Middle Ages, from about A.D. 200 to 500, the understanding of being called out and of being a fellowship still prevailed. Parallel to this, however, came the sense of the special roles of the hierarchy of the community as the reflection of the divine order and as the representative of the authority of God and Christ. When it became clear that the Second Coming was delayed, there were far-reaching changes in the character of the Christian Church. In particular, steps were taken to preserve orthodoxy. After all, because the Church was founded on a set of beliefs, it was absolutely essential to ensure that the fundamental faith not be lost or corrupted as it was handed on from one person to another.

This desire to preserve the pristine faith gave rise to the concept of apostolic succession. While the early Christians avoided using the term "priest," by the second century the bishops and presbyters became priests, in fact if not in name. For the first time, in the letter of Clement of Rome (c. A.D. 95), the term "laïkos" (derived from the Greek word "laos" or "people") was applied to the ordinary faithful in contrast to the officials of the Church. In the first century, the entire Church had seen itself as a holy group surrounded by a secular world; by the end of the fifth century, the clergy constituted a holy group within the Church, surrounded by a secular laity.

During the Middle Ages, from about A.D. 500 to 1500—the third period—two factors shaped the development of the clergy-laity relationship. The first was a gradual interweaving of the Church and civil society, and the second, the transfer of the tension and opposition between the Church and the world to within the Church itself. On the one hand, the Church, the one stable factor in the upheavals of the barbarian invasions, assumed the burden of upholding the earthly and political order among the young nations. This heightened the role of the officials of the Church to the point where they adopted the secular trappings of authority and power. On the other hand, because the distinction between Church and world had moved to within the Church itself, the truly spiritual man, such as the monk, was contrasted with the man who was occupied with the things of the world. True and authentic Christianity appeared, above all, as a detachment from the world. By necessity, the Church officials were engaged in pursuits one would now call "secular." To offset this, a variation of a monastic form of life was adopted, and the hierarchy became a distinct class.

Where did this leave the laity? Because they were not qualified to provide leadership in the world, the laity were excluded from the task of bringing form and order into the political and cultural wasteland that had once been the Western Empire. They lived in an arena that was in opposition to the Church, so they had to be saved and rescued by the Church. The ideal presented to the laity was more appropriate for someone living in a monastery rather than someone involved in the hustle and bustle of the world. The great representative of the laity was the prince and ruler, whose formation or education was taken very seriously, and whose work was regarded as a real service of the Church.

The laity were now reduced to a passive role. This was mirrored, above all, in the liturgy, which was performed by the clergy, while the ordinary faithful were reduced to a community of hearers.

The time after the Middle Ages and the period of the Reformation, from about A.D. 1500 to the present, can be described as an epoch of emancipation; the world is set free from the tutelage of the Church and becomes conscious of its own value and autonomy.

For the first time in history, the Church was confronted with the whole world. The first reaction of the Church was a defensive one. Its pastoral work was organized mainly to maintain little islands of the older Christendom within this new profane world. With the development of a fortress mentality, the hierarchy and intellectuals of the Church actively sought out the laity to help dominate a more and more complex world. As far as service to the Church was concerned, this was barely spelled out—only in terms of receiving a mandate from the bishops or participating in the apostolate of the hierarchy. This was more or less the state of affairs on the eve of Vatican II.

All this changed during the Council because of the emergence in the document *Lumen Gentium* of the pivotal image of "People of God." Since the time of the apostles, different images had been used to describe the Church: "flock," "body of Christ," "bride," "family of God," "institutional church." Vatican II restored the title "People of God" for the Church, in chapter 2 of *Lumen Gentium*. This title, validly founded in Scripture (1 Pt 2:9–10), met the desire of the Council to emphasize the human and communal side of the Church, rather than just the institutional and hierarchical aspects that where sometimes overstressed for polemical reasons. The Council wanted to emphasize that the Church is first and foremost people who believe that Jesus is the Lord. The unity of all members is founded on the common baptism, confirmation, and call of all, and on their participation in the triple office—king, prophet, priest—of Christ. This unity precedes all distinctions.

Chapter 2 of *Lumen Gentium* balanced this viewpoint with its emphasis that the People of God exists, in historical fact, as an articulated fellowship. It is safe to say that the title "People of God" implies an entirely different way of viewing the Church. This paves the way for the fourth chapter of *Lumen Gentium*, which discusses the special place of the laity in the Church as a whole. This chapter is in turn the basis of the *Decree on the Apostolate of the Laity, Apostolicam Actuositatem.*

Before Chapter 4 of *Lumen Gentium* was approved, it was subject to harsh criticism and to wholesale revisions. The first version of the chapter, which came before the Council Fathers in December 1962, considered the laity largely in relation to the hierarchy: it treated the priesthood of the believers as something less than a real priesthood; and it seemed to regard the world as closed, if not actually hostile, to the Gospel. In July 1963, the chapter on the laity, which had previously been chapter 6 in the schema on the Church, now appeared as chapter 3. During the course of the debate, some of the Council Fathers firmly opposed the ideas of what was clearly the majority. The members of this minority group seemed to regard the laity as a purely passive element in the Church, at best an instrument of the hierarchy, its executive organ in the secular sphere; they were prepared to view the relationship between the hierarchy and the laity in no other terms than those of authority and obedience.

The final arrangement that makes the chapter on the laity the fourth of the schema on the Church instead of the third is a felicitous one. The present arrangement ensures that the place of the ecclesiastical officer and layman in the Church is seen in due perspective; it also highlights the inner bond between individual members of the New Testament People of God and their office-bearers, and the fundamental equality of both as regards vocation, dignity, and commitment. No longer will it be such a temptation to consider those in the hierarchy, even individual office-bearers, as beings separate from the People of God—indeed, as absolute masters of their subjects. No longer will it be easy to talk of obedience and subordination only in connection with the laity, as if they had no status whatsoever.

What are the key elements of chapter 4 of *Lumen Gentium* and the *Decree on the Apostolate of the Laity*?

By placing the laity directly in the mission of the Church, the *Decree on the Apostolate of the Laity* set up a relationship with other major documents of the Council. The documents on the Church in the modern world, ecumenism, missionary life, Christian education, and the liturgy speak to the laity about their role in various areas of the Church's mission.

The laity are no longer viewed as the clients of the clergy. In fact, the Council places great emphasis on the relationship between pastors and laity. It exhorts the pastors to humility, since they must remember that "they themselves were not meant by Christ to shoulder alone the entire saving mission of the Church toward the world" (LG 30). The prerequisite for the fruitfulness of the work of the laity is their "living union with Christ": they must go to the pastors who are the servants of the word and ministers of the sacraments (AA 4, 28, 29). Contact with the laity can refresh the spirit of the pastors. They should listen willingly to the laity and allow them considerable freedom and initiative. Although the Council speaks about co-operation between clergy and laity, it does not use the term "collegiality" to describe relations between the hierarchy and the laity.

Lumen Gentium avoids a definition of laity: it gives instead a description first in negative and then in positive terms. Laymen are neither ordained nor under public vows. If the document rather negatively distinguishes the laity from people in the clerical or religious state, at least it describes them as believers in Christ. But it says other favourable things about them as well. The laity are incorporated in Christ by baptism, thus becoming members of the People of God and sharing in Christ's office as king, prophet, and priest. Furthermore, they share in that office in their own proper manner and carry out the mission of the whole Christian people in the Church and in the world in their own way (LG 31). Thus, what confers the rights and duties of the apostolate consists in one's belonging to a body of which Christ is the head and internal principle of life through his Spirit, and as such participating in the mission of Christ. The fundamental call to the ministry is therefore not a mandate given by the hierarchy.

To describe the activity of the laity, the Council uses the traditional expression "lay apostolate," but in a sense that departs so much from the original usage that it needs to be carefully explained to avoid restricting it to "spiritual co-operation." It identifies the apostolate with complete participation in executing the mission of the Church taken in all its fullness.

The *Decree on the Apostolate of the Laity* states that the ministry of the laity must include work in the Church as well as outside in the temporal world. The Council wanted to describe lay people as members of the Holy Church set apart and as active in the spiritual domain, whether in the liturgy, the apostolate, or charity. However, it is still true that lay Christians are, by their very situation, in a position to act on the temporal and to sanctify it from within. Although the priest has to help sanctify the temporal order by his own ministry, the laity affect the sanctification of the temporal order in a special way. The temporal order must be directed for its own sake as regards its own internal structures, in a Christian way and toward God; this is the work of the laity.

It is noteworthy that the exhortation to traditional works of charity is linked with a strong statement about efforts to remove the causes of poverty, injustice, and suffering (AA 8).

The decree is silent on several issues. It does not say anything about a share of the laity in the actual government of the Church, and it does not satisfactorily address the dilemmas of the modern Christians in their daily work.

How has the decree affected the life of the Church, particularly in Canada? The image of the People of God appeared to authorize lay independence from ecclesiastical control in worldly affairs. It also promised a larger role for lay people within the Church. In this respect, considerable progress has been made since the Council. A linguistic shift has developed that is likely to have far-reaching ramifications. The term "ministry" is used so pervasively now that it is the laity who are the generic category for ministry; ordained ministers are only a particular instance of the ministry shared by all Christians.

This notion of ministry is articulated in the context of a declining number of clerics throughout the world. What is at stake here is not only the meeting of leadership needs in the modern Church, but also the discovery of more appropriate relationships and actions between laity and clergy, Church and world. At the present time, our bishops demonstrate a growing openness to the involvement of lay people in Church activities of every sort. As the laity become more and more involved in the life of the Church, however, there will be problems and questions. Which activities of the laity are properly considered lay ministry? How are such ministries recognized and made official by the Church? Must they be so validated? What is their relationship to the ordained ministry of the clergy?

The Council did seek to elevate the status of the laity and to affirm that they were as essential to the Church as the clergy and those in religious communities. Nonetheless, it retained a strong sense of the separation, if not the inequality, of the two groups, by its stress on the worldly or secular character of lay life. It recognized that lay people are to exercise a genuine apostolate but that their activity belongs primarily in the secular realm, "penetrating and perfecting the temporal sphere of things through the spirit of the gospel." The laity must take on the renewal of the temporal order as their own special obligation (AA 2, 7).

The Council's emphasis on the secular character of the laity arose from its new-found regard for the world and the consequent need to maintain some tangible connection with it once the Church renounces its claims to direct power over it. By apparently acknowledging the world's autonomy and the benefits that the Church receives from the world, Vatican II signalled the end of the embattled relationship. Yet, despite its appreciation of the world, the Council could not conceive of the Church and the world as integrally related. The idea that there is or can be a Church apart from the world, a Church that in a pure setting of religious reflection defines its stance toward that world, is as misleading as the notion that nothing of religious significance exists beyond the Church unless Church people bring it there.

Vatican II's re-evaluation of Church and world—more like an updating of the pattern of medieval Christendom than the creation of a new, self-critical understanding and relationship—has led to an interesting situation. A renewal movement intended to encourage Catholic involvement in secular affairs has gradually but irresistibly led to an ever more intense concern for the integrity, vitality, and coherence of the Church itself. The laity, perhaps better than the office-bearers, see the Church in the world; any mandate to involve themselves in the affairs of the world is also a mandate to involve themselves in the affairs of the Church. Therefore, the challenge concerning the involvement of the laity in the temporal sphere in a meaningful way still remains. Just as it did twenty years ago, it requires knowledge of the world and how it works, and love for that world and the people who live in it. What needs to be developed is a strong pastoral social theology.

The promulgation of the new Code of Canon Law has brought to fruition the *Decree on the Apostolate of the Laity*. The Code has incorporated the doctrinal elements of *Apostolicam Actuositatem* (Canon 204), and spelled out in a number of canons the obligations and rights that belong to all the faithful (Canons 208–31). It has gone much further than a mere listing of rights and duties. Throughout the Code, it is clearly evident that the laity have the right and duty to participate actively in the Church's three-fold mission of governing, teaching, and sanctifying. The laity can now be given a real share in the government of the Church, particularly at the judicial and executive level; offices previously reserved to the clerics are now open to the faithful, both men and women.

Indeed, it is clear from the revised legislation that the laity are expected to take an active part in the general running of the Church, at both diocesan and parochial levels.

The new Code is a serious effort to recognize and support the function of the laity in the Church in accordance with the teaching of Vatican II. While it remains true that final decision making remains for the most part in the hands of the clergy, the new law does envisage that most decisions will involve serious consultation with the faithful, including the laity.

Since the close of the Council, the implementation of *Apostolicam Actuositatem* has continued apace. It is fair to say, however, that some issues still need to be urgently addressed—issues like the role of women in the Church, the relationship of lay people to the magisterium of the Church, and the reconciliation of the Church and world.

COMMENTARY ON THE

Dogmatic Constitution on Divine Revelation

Dei Verbum

GEORGE SCHNER

The final document of Vatican II on the subject of divine revelation, entitled *Dei Verbum*, the Word of God, occupies a unique place among the documents of the Second Vatican Council because of the history of its construction, the nature of the text itself, its doctrinal content, and its implications for Church relations, both internal and external.

The historical importance of the document and its relation to the work of the Council as a whole are succinctly expressed in the words of one Council Father, Archbishop Denis Hurley. Reflecting on the first session in 1962, which dealt with the first draft of the document, at that time entitled *The Two Sources of Revelation*, he stated:

> To few men is it granted to sit through such a debate as echoed around St. Peter's from November 14 to 21. That debate on *The Sources of Revelation* was vital because it would indicate whether or not the Church was willing to turn its back on the past in order to go unhindered into the future.
>
> When we filed out of St. Peter's on the 20th, many of us felt we had voted the end of an era. God knows it was time.[1]

Bishop Hurley's blunt statement may seem a harsh judgment on the Church of the late nineteenth and early twentieth centuries. He was not alone in his opinion; immediately after the close of the Council, many articles and books appeared on the content and significance of the *Dogmatic Constitution on Divine Revelation* that echoed his convictions.[2] Most consider the history of the construction of the text itself and the debate on the Council floor as essential to an understanding of the extraordinary significance of the text. In summarizing its doctrinal content, George Tavard, for example, states:

> In other words, the Revelation is neither essentially a doctrine, although it implies one, nor a set of propositions and formulations to be believed,

although it may be partially expressed in such propositions, nor the promulgation of an ethical law of prescriptions and proscriptions, although it also implies judgment of the morality of human behavior. Essentially, the Revelation is a life.[3]

Tavard here summarizes all the former notions of Revelation that were set aside in the Council document. The Council Fathers stressed the notion of Revelation as life—both the gift of God's life in the communication of God's Word, and the life of the Church in accordance with that gift.

The final text of the *Dogmatic Constitution on Divine Revelation* is both the historic act Archbishop Hurley sensed it to be, and the doctrinal statement Tavard carefully circumscribes. As the Theological Commission and the Council Fathers themselves constructed and amended the text, it came to express certain rules of thought and action that are not theological, ethical or procedural sentences, but rule-like sentences that govern Christian discourse and action as a whole. The Council Fathers integrated the practical experience of conducting such a gathering as a Council with the task of articulating foundations in a text. Thus, the history and content of the text are mutually illuminative. My essay will necessarily treat both.

HISTORY AND CONSTRUCTION OF THE TEXT

As early as November 1961, the Theological Commission, headed by Cardinal Ottaviani, with Sebastien Tromp, S.J., professor at the Gregorian University, as secretary, began its construction of a document on "the two sources of Revelation." The majority of the commission represented the thinking of what is called the manual tradition of theology, especially as represented by the Lateran University. That is to say, most members favoured the theological convictions of those who wrote the textbooks of theology, in Latin, to be used by seminaries around the world. Such textbooks usually ignored the more recent scholarship in theology and other disciplines. Those in the minority were sympathetic to the contemporary theological work of *resourcement* throughout the Catholic world of scholarship. They were unable to moderate the majority's preoccupation with condemnation of certain developments in Catholic scholarship. In keeping with the attack the Curia had made on the Biblical Institute in Rome in 1960, the original draft was highly critical of biblical scholarship. It was polemical against both the "new theology" developed in Europe in the 1950's and generally against anything other than Roman Catholic theological notions. The text was written with an abstract philosophical rendering of doctrinal issues, to the neglect of pastoral concerns. Despite the efforts of the minority, who were unwilling to put forward a constitution shaped by the manual tradition, and of the Secretariat for Promoting Christian Unity, which offered to help the Theological Commission but was ignored, the text entitled *The Two Sources of Revelation* was distributed to the Council Fathers in July 1962. As Bishop André Charue, a vice-president of the Theological Commission, stated, it was a text "couched in unduly scholastic terminology" and "not very ecumenical in tone."[4]

This judgment is clearly shown in the first draft, in its adherence to the theological theories that argue for a two-source theory of Revelation, a coincidence of tradition with the magisterium of the hierarchical Church, a literalist notion of the scriptural texts, a rejection of scholarly exegetical methods, and a rejection of a notion of doctrinal development.

The official draft was presented to the Council Fathers in the first session, on November 14, 1962. But there was already opposition to the document. A group of bishops circulated an unofficial document to some of the Council Fathers. This group included bishops from France, Germany, Belgium, Holland and Austria, and theologians like Karl Rahner and Joseph Ratzinger were among the authors. Cardinal Ottaviani made a spirited presentation of the official text, insisting on its necessity as a defence of truly Catholic doctrine. Immediately after, a series of scholars, including Leinart, Frings, Leger, Konig, Alfrink, Suenens and Bea, and ultimately bishops from every continent of the world, spoke against the document. Their criticisms, succinctly stated by the first person to speak, Cardinal Lienart, can be summarized as follows:

1. Two two-source theory is not the tradition of the Church but a particularly recent, Roman theological notion.
2. The style, language and theological notions used create a "cold and scholastic formula."
3. The document is not ecumenical.
4. The document is condemnatory rather than pastoral.

During the deliberations a vote was taken on November 20, 1962. Those in favour of interrupting the discussion of the schema were to vote Yes, those in favour of continuing the discussion were to vote No. The very wording of the question was not in keeping with the custom of the Council, where a vote generally indicated pleasure or displeasure with the text itself, not the discussion. Could this change in procedure have been an attempt by those favouring the text to confuse the Fathers of the Council? And confused they were. Announcements had to be made during the voting to help clarify the question. But some of these, especially one by Cardinal Ruffini, a staunch supporter of the schema, confused the issue even more. Nevertheless, the result of the vote, 1,368 against the text and 822 for it, was a victory in principle for what was to become the dominant view of the whole Council. It was not, however, the two-thirds majority needed to send the document automatically back to the commission. Pope John XXIII himself intervened, in effect acting upon the suggestions that had long come from the Secretariat for Promoting Christian Unity, from several bishops speaking during the debate, and specifically from Archibishop Garrone two days before. Pope John also reconstituted the Commission as a mixed one, with members from both the Theological Commission and the Secretariat for Promoting Christian Unity; he appointed Cardinals Bea and Ottaviani as co-presidents.

It was not until April 22, 1963 that this new commission presented a revised draft to the Council Fathers. It had considered more than three hundred submissions containing general comments and specific suggestions for textual emendations in the document. The discussion of it did not take place until the third session of the Council, when even more changes were suggested. The third draft was distributed in July 1964 and came to the floor for discussion on September 30, 1964. Once again, two introductions were made, one representing the opinion of those opposed to the new document, and one representing the majority's approval. This balance of opinion among the Council Fathers was a reversal of the views in the Theological Commission. Sixty-nine Fathers spoke on the document. No final vote was taken at this session. Once again, the Mixed Commission considered some two hundred suggested amendments but only a few were accepted.

It was only on September 20, 1965 that voting began on the fourth revised draft. The voting is significant for the final days' work on the text:

	Approval	Disapproval	Qualified Approval
Introduction and Chapter 1	1,822	3	248
Chapter 2	1,874	9	354
Chapter 3	1,777	6	324
Chapter 4	2,183	—	47
Chapter 5	1,850	—	313
Chapter 6	1,915	1	213

Though the revisions of the past two years had succeeded in articulating the general convictions of the Council Fathers, it was clear that some Fathers still had reservations about certain phrases and sentences; this is evident in their qualified approval. Before the final vote, they made further amendments, three at the suggestion of Pope Paul VI himself.

It is instructive to note that these final amendments were made to the major doctrinal chapters, chapters 2 and 3, and to chapter 5 on the New Testament. They concerned the question of the material extent of tradition itself, the nature of the inerrancy of the Scriptures, and the historicity of the gospel accounts. At last, a series of "final" votes was taken, the very last taking place on the day of the promulgation of the *Dogmatic Constitution on Divine Revelation*, November 18, 1965; 2,344 Council Fathers were in favour and only 6 opposed.

This brief summary of how the text came to be describes a rehearsal of the major themes of the new and final text. Indirectly, the text is about the movement away from a scholastic theology and its highly intellectualistic articulation of doctrine, and as such a movement away from the domination of conciliar documents by any one theological school of thought. Second, it is about the movement away from a defensive and condemnatory attitude toward an ecumenical and pluralistic articulation of the Church's identity and purpose. It is about the doctrine of Revelation and the foundation of Christian thought and action in its one source, the Word of God.

ANALYSIS OF THE TEXT

The final text is divided into a preface and six chapters. The initial three chapters expanded what had been only a preface and two chapters in the first version and changed the content significantly. The order and subject matter of the last three remained the same in all five versions of the text, namely the chapters on the Old Testament, the New Testament, and Sacred Scripture in the life of the Church. The tone and style of all the chapters changed from the first version, in part because Scripture texts informed its vocabulary and imagery rather than being invoked as proof texts or simple quotations. Such changes were required by the radical shift in content and attitude of the whole Council. But the change was by no means complete, given the nature of the debate by the Council Fathers and the inevitable difficulties of constructing a document in a committee.

PREFACE

The three sentences of the preface illustrate the basic themes and problems of the whole text. The beginning phrase "Hearing the word of God" states the topic of the text: Revelation is but one thing, the Word of God; all further distinctions will be referred to that one source. The rest of the first sentence is a quotation from 1 Jn 1:2–3, a succinct statement of Christian kerygma and ministry. As a rule that stands over the entire document, it does not summarize the text, since the document not kerygmatic but doctrinal. Moreover, it does not state the entire message, but concentrates upon its foundation in the Word of God.

The second sentence continues the confusion between preaching the Word of God and giving a doctrinal account of that Word. First, it states the material content of the document ("authentic teaching about divine revelation and about how it is handed on")[5] and its character as a development in continuity with Trent and Vatican I. Then, however, the sentence states that the purpose of such teaching is kerygmatic.

This contradiction can be resolved if the references to kerygma are taken to express the purpose of the document as a whole, and therefore of the work of the Council. Their purpose is not to adjudicate scholarly theological disputes or to be preoccupied with self-definition. The demand to be pastoral and ecumenical precludes both, and the radical changes in the content and style of the text suggest serious efforts to satisfy both demands. If this is indeed the case, then in a halting way the Council tried to construct a statement that is doctrinal, pastoral and beyond allegiance to any particular theological school. Though they may not have been aware of it, the Council Fathers and their theological experts provided us with a document that now can be seen as distinctly innovative. This interpretation of the whole text allows me to examine it for what I will call the rules of grammar for Christian speech and action.[6]

CHAPTER 1

In the first chapter, the subject of the text—Revelation—is defined as the manifestation of God as Creator and Lord of human history, in the person and work of Jesus Christ, ever more fully grasped by us through the work of the Holy Spirit. This articulation of the trinitarian character of Christian Revelation points to the first rule of Christian discourse: God and God's acts must be spoken of as hidden yet revealed, incarnate and historical "through Christ, the Word made flesh," and charismatic "in the Holy Spirit" (2). This three-fold language is visible throughout the document, requiring constant qualification of formulations. Second, there is a clear Christocentrism. The person and work of Christ are considered both the norm and standard for revelation and salvation. In effect, this is a further specification of the first rule.

Third, there is the requirement for what I will call a "narrative" articulation in Christian language: in the words of the text this "plan of revelation is realized by deeds and words having an inner unity" (2). The entire text itself obeys this rule with its constant use of descriptive narrative in the course of definition. By articulating and following these three rules, the Council constructed a text that "has remained outside all technical theological positions."[7]

A fourth rule of discourse is not adequately followed in the text: an account of the word of salvation must always take into account the sinful character of humanity. The text has an overly optimistic tone in its account of salvation history and an all too brief reference to the sinful character of humanity in the phrase "[t]hen after the fall" (3). This tone in the text was noted by the Council Fathers themselves and in subsequent commentaries on the text.[8]

Finally, the movement of the text itself in chapter 1 suggests a priority of language about God over the language of Christian anthropology; it is only in the fifth article that the response of the human person is noted. What must first be stated and what is of greatest importance are the acts of God.

Article 5 also shows, however, the not altogether successful attempt to replace scholastic terminology ("submission of intellect and will") with narrative language. The reference to faith as knowledge, joined with a statement of faith as trust and obedience, seems to be opportune. If the text had followed one of Karl Barth's discussions of faith[9] and proceeded to speak of faith as confession, the chapter could have closed with a remark aptly transitional to the next chapter. Instead, the text refers to "the grace of God and the interior help of the Holy Spirit" (5) and reiterates faith as a matter of understanding. This preference for understanding rather than confession of one's faith comes from the close adherence of this part of the text to the text of Vatican I, *Dogmatic Constitution on the Catholic Faith,* which emphasized the intellectual assent necessary in faith. However, what this present text omits from the text of Vatican I is highly significant, namely any reference to external arguments as "proofs" for faith.

If the text had ended with reference to faith as confession, article 6 would not have been necessary. As it stands, it is an attempt to insert some sentences to address matters inappropriate at this point, namely the problem of contemporary atheism and the response of Christians in theological apologetics.

The problems involved here are the complex issues that theologians are currently discussing concerning the existence and nature of fundamental or foundational theology.[10] They also require an analysis of contemporary culture, aided by the social sciences and philosophy, with a view to establishing just how the Church and its faith can illuminate our culture and its problems. Article 6 asserts, on the one hand, the transcendent character of Revelation ("divine treasures which totally transcent the understanding of the human mind" 6), and on the other hand, the rationality of Revelation ("religious truths which are by their nature accessible to human reason" 6). Both assertions are true of Christian speech and action; however, they repeat the rules already contained in the Trinitarian, Christocentric and narrative requirements set forth in the first three articles of this chapter. Moreover, atheism and apologetics are not matters of arguments about rationality but the confrontation of faiths. Those constructing the text grasped that point: they omitted any reference to the so-called external arguments of miracles and prophecy in article 5.

CHAPTER 2

The second chapter develops the manner of the transmission of the Revelation of God in both Scripture and tradition. The first part of article 7 follows the rules set down in the first chapter. It establishes the nature of tradition by a narrative of the preaching, example, law giving and writing of the apostles and their companions, grounded in the providence of God through the fulfilment in Christ, and the prompting of the Holy Spirit. The second part, in one brief sentence, links tradition with the office of teaching, visible in the succession of apostles and bishops.

The next and final sentence of the paragraph hints at the limitation of tradition as the act of a pilgrim Church awaiting fulfilment in the eschaton. The first chapter failed to observe adequately the rule requiring the sinful dimension of humanity to be included in any articulation of Christian belief. In a similar way, this sentence remains a mere cipher for a serious problem with the entire discussion of tradition: the lack of any accommodation for a Church activity critical of tradition itself.

The beginning of article 8 does advert indirectly to the possibility of a divergence from orthodoxy and orthopraxis in "teaching, life, and worship." However, in the phrase "fight in defense of the faith," it implies that the dangers are from outside the community, even though the reference to 2 Thes 2:15 refers to a controversy that is within the Church. This sentence is the only place in the document where the subject matter is referred to in the plural—"traditions." The existence and consequences of pluralism in the Church are not dealt with again at this point. If they had been, the text could then have offered criteria by which any one tradition could be judged to be fundamentally out of harmony with the Christian faith.

The Council Fathers themselves observed both the rule of trinitarian discourse as well as the rule of human fallibility; several speeches adverted directly to these matters. Of note are the comments by Bishop Edelby on the inseparability of the work of Father, Son and Holy Spirit from the use of the Scriptures, and the comments of Cardinal Meyer of Chicago on the fallibility of tradition in a pilgrim Church.[11]

The remaining two paragraphs of article 8 reveal yet another confusion: the difference between the development of dogma and the dynamic character of tradition itself (as comprising a pluralism of Church life). That two Council Fathers of highly divergent views, Cardinals Ruffini and Leger, could both speak against these paragraphs suggests that these two quite different notions are confused in these sentences.[12] The commission assigned with the task of amending the text according to the suggestions of the Fathers was satisfied that the text did not imply that Revelation itself was somehow still developing,[13] nor was the living presence of the Holy Spirit properly to be called Revelation.

It would take a very careful analysis of such phrases as "the Church constantly moves forward toward the fullness of divine truth" (8) to make them acceptable to all partners in an ecumenical dialogue or, more fundamentally, consonant with the rule set out in the first chapter that Revelation is fulfilled in the person and work of Christ. The many suggested last-minute revisions to this paragraph, and particulartly to its final addition, show that the Council Fathers were aware that serious matters were not resolved by the present formulation. On the other hand, if the word "truth" were not read to mean the truth of propositions, and if the eschatological theme of the sentence were heightened (as in a previous form of the text that indicated references to 1 Cor 13:30 and Rv 17:17), then the sentence could be understood as in keeping with the rest of the text.

Article 9 asserts that the unity of Scripture and tradition is founded in the Word of God. In doing so, it sets aside the theory that was the heart of the first text, *De Duplice Fontes*. However, issues that separate the major concerns of the Church are not resolved by the last-minute addition of the sentence, "Consequently, it is not from sacred Scripture alone that the Church draws her certainty about everything which has been revealed" (10) and the final sentence urging equal "devotion and reverence" (10) for both Scripture and tradition. A tendency still remains to revert to a consideration of tradition as materially different from Scripture. The last-minute insertion was clearly done to satisfy those Council Fathers unwilling to abandon allegiance to only one school of theology.

Article 10 relates the unity of Scripture and tradition to the "living teaching office of the Church" and places the three-fold unity "under the action of the one Holy Spirit." In the course of doing so, some controversial issues are touched upon: the relation of oral and written tradition; the development of tradition; the unity of Scripture and tradition; and the relation of both to the magisterium. It is evident in article 10 that tradition is not to be equated with the teaching office of the Church. It is also clear that this office is at the service of the Word of God, not above it. What remains confused are the distinctions I have already noted, and still unobserved is the rule about human fallibility. Therefore, the possibility that tradition could go astray needs to be considered.

To put the matter in a different way, if Scripture and tradition are seen as parallel, what notion is parallel to inerrancy? Is it infallibility? If so, in what sense can tradition be called infallible? These questions cannot be answered clearly if tradition is confused with the development of dogma, or if the plurality of traditions in the Church is not distinguished from tradition understood as the handing on of the Christian way of life.

The remaining four chapters take the Scriptures as their topic directly, beginning with the matter of divine inspiration and the interpretation of texts in general. The final text sets aside the initial preoccupation of the Theological Commission to discuss these related issues in terms of the inerrancy of the Scriptures and the dangers of contemporary biblical exegesis. As commentators point out, the final text is clearly accepting of contemporary biblical criticism, and leaves the details of such scholarly work to the biblical experts.

CHAPTER 3

This chapter enunciates certain rules about the truth value and the use of the Scriptures themselves. The Council Fathers struggled considerably over these two issues, as is clear from the speeches and written submissions of the third session, the many suggestions for detailed changes offered at the voting in September 1965, and the intervention of Pope Paul VI urging a revision of the text's definition of the truth of the Scripture texts. This struggle resulted in a final edition of the text that affirms and encourages the work of contemporary bibilical exegetes. It is notable the text does not give a psychological explanation in the discussion of either inspiration or interpretation. It is content with rule-like statements, which themselves are in keeping with the rules set down in the previous chapters.

The text explains inspiration by using a narrative of origins, speaking of a choice by God, mentioning several times the work of the Holy Spirit, and ending in article 13 with an analogy between the Scripture text and the incarnation of the Son, parts requiring the expression of the transcendent in the frailty and weakness of the human. In some sense the discussion of rules for interpretation in article 12 adheres to the rule about human frailty. These parts of chapter 3 seem to follow the rule articulated earlier in the text, that all discourse about Revelation and its embodiment take into account the fallen sinful character of humanity. What is needed is some statement of the fallibility of interpretation; given the intransigence of some, the theological advisors and more enlightened Council Fathers had to give a strong statement of approval for contemporary biblical exegesis.

If we consider carefully only two sentences of this chapter, we can see the purpose of the text as a compendium of rules. They are not, of course, the rules of hermeneutics or philosophy, since the Council Fathers were not convened as experts on the methodology of biblical scholarship. Rather, they are stating what is "subject finally to the judgment of the Church" (12), namely the truth and meaning of the Scriptures. In the words suggested by Paul VI and adopted by the Mixed Commission, it is "that truth which God wanted put into the sacred writings for the sake of our salvation" (11). And in the next article, it is "what God wanted to communicate to us" (12) that the interpreter must seek out. This truth is neither equated with nor subordinate to the "meaning the sacred writers really intended" (12), and therefore the interpretation of Scripture does not presuppose a coincidence of absolute truth with the verbal content of the Scriptures. Rather, the text offers two rules: all these sentences of Scripture articulate saving truths; and all these sentences articulate human truth. Like the sentence "Let's play ball!", these rules do not settle matters. They are only the beginning of the work to be done.[14] The great advantage of speaking about inspiration and interpretation in this way is its avoidance of a particular psychological or theological theory.

CHAPTER 4

This chapter affirms the intrinsic worth of the Old Testament and relates it to the whole plan of salvation and therefore to the New Testament texts. It is noteworthy that, while the text itself obeys the three rules already discussed, it does not present any detailed rules of hermeneutics for the Old Testament, except to describe the general content of these books. Most commentators agree that the Council Fathers were aware that the papal encyclical *Divino Afflante Spiritu* had presented sufficient material in this regard; therefore, further specification was not necessary.[15] The general rule for theology and piety found here is an assertion that the books of the Old Testament "written under divine inspiration, remain permanently valuable" (14) and that "Christians should receive them with reverence" (15).

CHAPTER 5

This chapter addresses the New Testament, especially the pre-eminence of the gospels and their character, as both historical and literary constructions. It begins with article 17, added late in the construction of the text, which, following the rule for narrative, locates the New Testament within the history of God's acts. It is in the writings of the New Testament that the Word of God "is set forth and shows its power in a most excellent way."

What the next three articles do *not* say is as important as what they do say. Leaving behind the polemical and unecumenical tone and style of the original schema, the text abandons the notions of textual positivism and naive historicism that all the gospels are eye-witness accounts, for example. Instead, the Mixed Commission constructed a chapter that asserts the following: the apostolic origins of the gospels, without specifying matters of authorship; the historical character of the texts (in a phrase added in the very final amendments of the text, at the urging of Paul VI, to satisfy those Fathers who were afraid the text was not clear enough on the matter); and the character of the gospels as human constructions.

Perhaps once again there is unnecessary detail in this last matter; it is significant, however, that the source for much of article 19 was the instruction of the Pontifical Biblical Commission, *Santa Mater Ecclesia*. That instruction, at least in part, grew out of the necessity for the defence of Catholic biblical exegesis and the education of the Council Fathers. Its inclusion in the document is an effort to give legitimacy and authority to theological work that some Council Fathers considered dangerous or simply wrong.

The final article asserts the status of the rest of the New Testament as inspired but dependent upon the gospel stories. The final sentence of the chapter once again states the trinitarian origins of the New Testament, and does so in a narrative fashion: "For the Lord Jesus was with His apostles as He had promised (Mt 28:20) and sent to them as Paraclete the spirit who would lead them into the fullness of truth (Jn 16:13).

CHAPTER 6

In its first sentence, chapter 6 asserts the centrality of the Scriptures to the life of the Church, most strikingly by setting the Scriptures in parallel with the Eucharist. It insists that this principle must be at work in the whole Church: in the task of theological construction, in the liturgy, in the education of the clergy, and in the life of the laity. To put this principle in action, it is necessary to have the same growth beyond polemical and counter-reformation attitudes, toward the ecumenical and evangelical ones that the previous chapters required.

This final chapter states that the scholarly, education, liturgical and devotional changes necessary so that the new-found emphasis on the Word of God in the Scriptures will be realized in the life of the Church.

The text of the document ends therefore where the next section of this essay must begin. The questions remain: How has this document been received? And what effects has it had on the life of the Church?

IMPLEMENTATION

If my interpretation of the text as an effort at the statement of rules of Christian discourse is correct, then the text must be seen as demanding certain fundamental changes in theological construction and other practices of Church life. First, the text requires that the discussion of Revelation, as the Word of God, not be relegated to a single "treatise" but be the focus of all theological construction. This requires a reconsideration of the whole notion of theological foundations and the way matters of the authority of Scripture and tradition are discussed.

Second, the text requires that the Word of God, as expressed in the Scriptures, become normative for theological construction. That normativity can be expressed in the three general types of rules noted above, calling for trinitarian, narrative and fallible discourse. Third, in dialogue with these two activities is the general restructuring of liturgical, educational and devotional practice in the Church as a whole.

Many texts from the other documents of Vatican II show that the Council Fathers recognized and set in motion these very activities. They are in relation with the former ones; as they are fully engaged, they will make the theological changes necessary and possible. Those changes will further the changes of Church life and practice.

This accounts in part for my conviction that the document *Dei Verbum* is the most fundamental of the Council's documents. In asking for a reassessment of the basic rules of Christian discourse and action, involving a re-appropriation of the place of Scripture in the life of the Catholic Church, the Council Fathers were indeed taking seriously Pope John's request for a pastoral and ecumenical Council. In succeeding, at least in part, in constructing a document theologically neutral, all pervasive changes were necessary.

We have seen in North America, as elsewhere in the Church, the developments following the basic liturgical changes introduced after the Council, like the growth in Bible study groups, the adoption of a style of preaching with a greater emphasis on preaching "from the text." With the heightened awareness of the Scriptural texts, there has been greater appeal to Scripture as the authorization for any number of social and political ativities now undertaken in the name of Christian belief.

While efforts by scholars of theology and by theological institutions have tried to effect the first two changes I noted, the change in these areas is not yet fully in accord with the implications of the document we have been considering. Of course, neither have the developments in liturgical, devotional or ethical life been entirely satisfactory. Matters of theological education are, however, more acute since it is in such institutions that the ministers and leaders of the Church are formed. Any number of practical suggestions might follow from this judgment, which are topics for another and longer essay.[16]

Is all of this very much different from the aftermath of any of the Councils of the Church? In conclusion, let me cite one interesting and pertinent example.[17] At the close of the Council of Trent, the Council Fathers' insistence on the reform of theological education was carried out by the establishment of new procedures of study for clerics. One of the inventions was a course of study that surveyed the whole of Christian doctrine, developing examples and argumentation from the Scriptures and from patristic sources, and leaving aside the sterility of scholastic argumentation. Such a course was ultimately called fundamental theology. As the intellectual climate of Western Europe changed, the character of this course of study also changed. It constantly sought to meet the challenges of the day, whether they were deist arguments against the rationality of religion, arguments put forward against the truth and uniqueness of Catholicism or Christianity in the nineteenth century, or more recent atheistic arguments against any belief in God at all.

What Vatican II strongly recommended was, in many respects what Trent had also been interested in: a rediscovery of the Word of God as the norm for Church life and teaching. After four hundred years, the Church has returned to the importance of the Scriptures. Our efforts to accomplish that return will undoubtedly have unexpected results.

Notes

1. D. W. Hurley, "End of an Era," *Catholic Mind*, 61, 36.

2. The following is a brief list of sources. In the references listed under R. Latourelle and H. Vorgrimler, ample further material is to be found in footnotes and bibliography.

 The Bible Today, 35 (1968), 2418–60. The first six articles of this issue are commentaries on each of the chapters of the document.

 "The Vatican Council on Divine Revelation: An Interview with Abbot Butler," *The Clergy Review*, 50 (1965), 659–70.

 G. Baum, "Vatican II's Constitution on Revelation: History and Interpretation," *Theological Studies*, 28 (1967), 51–75.

 D. G. Bloesch, "Reader Response: The Constitution on Divine Revelation," *Journal of Ecumenical Studies*, 4 (1967), 550–51.

 P. W. Collins, "The Church and Revelation: A Development," *The American Ecclesiastical Review*, 167 (1973), 331–42.

 A. Dulles, "The Constitution on Divine Revelation in Ecumenical Perspective," *The American Ecclesiastical Review*, 154 (1966), 217–31.

 R. Latourelle, *Theology of Revelation* (Staten Island, N.Y.: Alba House, 1966).

 J. H. Miller, ed., *Vatican II: An Interfaith Appraisal* (Notre Dame and London: University of Notre Dame Press, 1967), 43–88.

 J. A. O'Flynn, "Notes and Comments: The Constitution on Divine Revelation," *The Irish Theological Quarterly*, 33 (1966), 254–65.

 Roger Schutz and Max Thurian, *Revelation: A Protestant View* (New York: Newman Press, 1968).

 G. H. Tavard, "Commentary on *De Revelatione*," *Journal of Ecumenical Studies*, 3 (1966), 1–35.

 H. Vorgrimler, ed., *Commentary on the Documents of Vatican II* (Freiburg: Herder, 1968), 155–272.

 T. Worden, "Revelation and Vatican II," *Scripture*, 19 (1967), 54–62.

3. G. H. Tavard, "Commentary on *De Revelatione*, 8.

4. Cited in *American Participation in the Second Vatican Council*, ed. V.A. Yzermans (New York: Sheed and Ward, 1967), 95.

5. All references to the *Dogmatic Constitution on Divine Revelation* are to A. P. Flannery, ed., *The Documents of Vatican II* (New York: Pillar Books, 1975).

6. This particular construal of the nature of doctrine and religion is presented by G. Lindbeck, *The Nature of Doctrine* (Philadelphia: The Westminster Press, 1984). In this essay, I will refer to the three models of religion and doctrine that Lindbeck describes. One is the congnitivist propositional model, in which religion and doctrine are conceived of as truth claims about objective realities. Another is the experiential expressivist model, in which religion and doctrine are conceived of as expressions of personal spiritual experi-

ence. And finally, there is the cultural linguistic model, in which religion and doctrine are conceived of as consisting of a culture and language that shape life and thought.

8.   J. Ratzinger, "Chapter I: Revelation Itself," in *Commentary on the Documents of Vatican II*, ed. H. Vorgrimler (Freiburg: Herder, 1968), 173.

9.   See Ratzinger, "Revelation Itself," 173f.

10.   K. Barth, *Dogmatics in Outline*, chaps. 1–4 (New York: Harper and Row, 1959).

11.   For an excellent history and reconstruction of these problems, see F. Fiorenza, *Foundational Theology* (New York: The Crossroads Publishing Co., 1984).

12.   See *Acta Synodalia Sacrosancti Concilii Vaticani II*, vol. 3, pt. 3 (Typis Polyglottis Vaticanis, 1974), 150–51, 306–09.

13.   For a discussion on some details, see Ratzinger, "Revelation Itself," 184–90. Even the footnote 19 in the Abbott edition of the *Documents* confuses tradition with the development of dogma.

14.   See *Acta Synodalia Sacrosancti Concilii Vaticani II*, vol. 4. pt. 5 (Typis Polyglottis Vaticanis, 1974), 696–97, 722–23.

15.   See A. Grillmeier, "The Divine Inspiration and the Interpretation of Sacred Scripture," in *Commentary on the Documents of Vatican II*, ed. H. Vorgrimler, vol. 3, 240–45. It is interesting to compare the suggestions given by Grillmeier, that two groups of rules are given in chapter 3, with the work of D. Kelsey, *The Uses of Scripture in Recent Theology* (Philadelphia: Fortress Press, 1975), especially chap. 5.

16.   Pius XII, *Divino Afflante Spiritu*, Sept. 30, 1943. This encyclical set down the basic principles of biblical exegesis which were to guide Catholic scholars.

17.   Such an essay would discuss the character of theological education, the importance of formation in that education, and a conceptualization of formation as the learning of the rules of grammar for Christian discourse and action, from within a cultural linguistic notion of religion and doctrine. Such an education would be in keeping with the fundamental principles I have shown to be at work in *Dei Verbum*. See my essay "Formation as a Unifying Concept of Theological Education," *Theological Education*, 21, no. 2, 94–113.

18.   See Fiorenza, *Foundational Theology*, chap. 9.

COMMENTARY ON THE

Constitution on the Sacred Liturgy

Sacrosanctum Concilium

ATTILA MIKLOSHAZY

G.P. Schner: I recall that you began speaking at the symposium by referring to the origins of the document on the liturgy.
A. Mikloshazy: Yes. The document was the result of the liturgical movement of the twentieth century, and the historical and theological research that this movement involved. Much of the document reflects the changes already asked for by the Liturgical Congresses held throughout the world in the twenty years prior to the Council. When the Fathers and their theological advisors came to the Council, they were to be presented with a draft well prepared by the preparatory commission.

It is interesting to note that from being fifth in position for discussion, the draft was moved to the first place in the first session. Pope John XXIII had clearly stated that the Council was to have a pastoral emphasis. Those responsible for the organization of the first session seem to have had the conviction that, since it is in the liturgy itself that the renewal of the Church is primarily promoted, this pastoral aim would be best advanced by the renewal of the liturgy itself. Moreover, the immediate production of a document on liturgical renewal would give the Council Fathers a sense of achievement.

A great deal of debate was not expected. This was in fact the case, and the *Sacrosanctum Concilium* was voted on in the second session in 1963.

But in post-conciliar discussion this apparent advantage was often cited as a major disadvantage of the document. As the first fruit of the Council's discussions, the document on the liturgy had not benefited from the lengthy debates on the nature and work of the Church in the following sessions. If a renewed liturgy is to shape the life of the Church, it should be based upon the reconsideration of ecclesiology that was to occupy a great deal of the Council's time.

GPS: Is it not the case, though, that the antecedent historical and theological research that was part of the liturgical movement was already developing this new ecclesiology?

AM: Yes, indeed. In the years before the Council, the role of the faithful in the Church and its liturgy was being given special attention, and the image of the Mystical Body was being developed. However, the document does not speak of the other models of the Church, especially as the People of God; nor does it emphasize such aspects as collegiality, which became an important factor in the Church's self-definition. Nonetheless, both the liturgical movement and the growing interest in biblical and patristic studies in the early part of the twentieth century were already the sources of the Council and its language and thought.

GPS: Do you think the fact that these movements had their origin in Europe prevented the document that resulted at the Council from addressing the needs of the Church elsewhere, especially in Africa and Asia?

AM: The emphasis on enculturation and the role of the local Church is itself largely a post-conciliar development, though the Council did emphasize a certain decentralization. The introduction of the vernacular in the liturgy, however, is clearly a statement of the importance of the local, regional Churches. The full significance of this was undoubtedly not realized. Its effects are just now being understood, and the problems related to it are being dealt with.

GPS: Let's turn to the text itself now, and consider what it has to say.

AM: The text, *Sacrosanctum Concilium*, consists of seven chapters and an appendix. Its most important feature is that, for the first time in the history of the Church, such a conciliar document deals with the theology of the liturgy. This has never been done before. Usually the liturgy was dealt with as to its history, or within a discussion of the sacraments, but not as to its own proper theology.

This theology of the liturgy emphasizes several things: first, the theocentric and salvation historical character of the liturgy; second, the importance of the Word of God, such an emphasis being due, undoubtedly, to the ecumenical movement of this century; third, the Christocentric character of the liturgy as the Pascal Mystery and the presence of Christ in its manifold ways, as opposed to an exclusive emphasis on the Eucharistic presence; fourth, the ecclesial aspect of the liturgy, stressing a preference for the communal celebration of the liturgy as the work of the whole Christian people. The document gave a synthetic view of these characteristics in articles X to Y.

As for practical matters, the document states the need for formation in liturgical matters. It had been a motto of the entire liturgical movement that the faithful should take an active part in the liturgy. If this is to be possible, there must be preparation and education of the faithful through a great variety of means in both the parish and the diocese. Most especially, there must be an education of the clergy in liturgical matters. The document urged that a study of the liturgy become a major discipline in theological schools, just as dogmatic and moral theology are now. This, of course, did not occur, and the degree of instruction for the faithful varied greatly from place to place.

Nevertheless, the Holy See did issue extensive liturgical instructions after the Council to guide a renewal on the pastoral level. This was the beginning of the reform of the liturgical rites and practices which was to occupy the next ten years. The Consilium Liturgicum undertook to revise all of the rites in accord with historical research, principles and pastoral sensitivity. The work was done with wide consultation and with the help of many experts in these areas.

GPS: Just how was this reform carried out?

AM: Thousands of suggestions sent to the preparatory commission were gathered together by the Consilium Liturgicum. These experts from all parts of the world discussed each rite, drew up proposals, and eventually submitted the revised forms to a special commission of bishops and cardinals. The final texts were ultimately approved by the Holy Father. Previously, all the revised texts had been sent to the bishops of the world in three editions: first, the "green" book, a second revised "white" book, and then the suggested final edition. Each time, the new suggestions for modification were discussed and incorporated where possible.

GPS: Actually, in many cases, the first or second revision was tried out, experimented with, on the local level.

AM: Yes. That is a good instance of how the participation of the faithful and the local Church was brought to bear on the work of the theological, historical and pastoral experts who were constructing the texts.

This was not without its problems, however. Many people were reluctant to accept anything new. Second, there was a lack of the instruction and catechesis that ought to have preceded any of the changes. In some cases, the new rites were simply imposed without any instruction as to what was being changed and why; these met with opposition. The third problem was the lack of leadership in liturgical matters, in part because the competent people were so occupied with producing the new texts that they did not have the time to work in their various local Churches to help enact the reform.

Thus, even though there were very enthusiastic people on the local level, they were often lacking the proper formation. As a result, what was asked for and even done by some was not always in keeping with the intended reform.

You might say there were two extremes: those who did not want to reform anything; and those who wanted to change a great deal but without sound principles or pastoral sense. This situation often created turmoil and uneasiness in the years immediately following the Council. I might call this the liturgical "revolution," whether for or against the reform. Both cases were without proper guidance.

Some experimentation became chiefly efforts at entertainment, a notion derived from the emphasis on entertainment in contemporary culture, especially in the arts. While experimentation was necessary, there were no clear guidelines on its limitation and evaluation. It was never easy to return to previous forms or move on to improved forms once the experimentation had run its course.

GPS: In the period of reform, then, both principles of the document were at work, namely, sound theological arguments and active participation by the faithful. But the difficulties arose in just how these two elements work together.

AM: The problems were not to be found just in the liturgical reform but also in the new emphasis on the reading of the Scriptures and in the new model of Church life which the Council set forth. It is not enough to produce a beautiful document; it requires very patient, even tedious, catechetical work for several decades to achieve results. So, we should not be surprised that we did not reach a point of complete reform within a few years after the Council. The work of a Council, as history teaches us, may require a hundred years for its effects to be realized.

GPS: What are some of these problems in the Church's efforts to reform the liturgy?

AM: I must say, first of all, that the problems are not entirely due to the excesses of individuals or the simple lack of leadership. They are the problems of the Church in all its aspects, and of our contemporary culture as well. This is not surprising, since the liturgy, as the focal point of the life and meaning of the Church, always manifests the current state of both Church and world in general. Christians bring themselves to the Sunday liturgy just as they are, and their concerns and the state of the world and the Church are made manifest.

GPS: As, for example, some people call the Prayers of the Faithful the editorial section of the Mass, where often opposing concerns and opinions are voiced.

AM: Yes, the "daily news." Now, this sort of element is necessary, but often it is evidence of the very problems of contemporary culture. One problem of particular importance is the loss of a sense of the sacred, of mystery. In our present secular culture, it is difficult for people to find God, or at least, to find God where Christians were accustomed to. Moreover, there is a demand to conform to our culture without any critique of it. It is a complex problem—this whole matter of a definition and diagnosis of just what our many-faceted contemporary culture is and how it should be understood. In fact, we are not dealing with a single unified culture at all.

The liturgy does not exist in a vacuum. The question must be asked, what culture and then what aspects within that culture do you want to associate the liturgical celebration with? The actions and language of the celebration will reflect the living culture of the participants, but the liturgy cannot simply adopt the ephemeral fads of a single group or a short period of time. There must be an effort to embody in the liturgy the more lasting values of the culture.

GPS: In the present, then, it is especially difficult when culture itself redefines what is authentic as the ephemeral, as the "throwaway," the spontaneous. You are suggesting, however, that the liturgy must be in touch with the culture but must also not give itself over to the demands of culture, particularly our present one.

AM: Another term associated with this is "relevance." There is a sense of urgency about being relevant, of creating instant successes or depth of feeling or insight into the meaning of things. Those responsible for the liturgy can attempt to conform to these demands. In effect, what is enacted simply confirms the loss of the sense of the sacred that I have been speaking about.

This awareness of the presence of God, of the awesome character of what is said and done, cannot be set aside if the liturgy is to be anything more than a trivial affair, a merely human event. In this sense, if the liturgy loses its sense of the sacred, then human culture itself has lost one of its essential aspects. The loss of the sense of the sacred in the liturgy is the impoverishment of the human spirit.

GPS: To summarize, then, if the liturgy is to accomplish one of its purposes, namely to be a critique of the human condition, then it cannot simply adopt the values, goals and habits of contemporary culture.

AM: A second problem is a lack of familiarity with the use of the symbols essential to the action of the liturgy. One can notice a certain kind of "spiritism" that does not appreciate the external manifestations, the symbolic gestures, ritual actions and verbal formulas; it wishes to do everything in the liturgy in an invisible, spiritual way. At the extreme, it is a kind of neo-montanism which over-emphasizes the spiritual and almost despises the material. Symbols, of course, are an inseparable unity of spirit and matter.

GPS: This tendency is also evident in the way in which spirituality can be narrowed to mean only the mystical sorts of spiritual life. Once again, a particular problem in the liturgical life of the Church—in this case, an over-emphasis of one essential feature, namely interiority—is symptomatic of a larger problem for the whole of Church life.

AM: Yes. It is also reminiscent of a certain Enlightenment attitude to

101

the liturgy as primarily a didactic tool that aims at moral instruction of the congregation. What seems to be at work in both attitudes is a lack of understanding of the symbol as having meaning in itself. Instead, a certain pragmatism enters, which urges that all gestures, practices and use of concrete symbols like colours or objects be judged as to their usefulness and disposed of accordingly. Once again, this is not a matter of a problem for the Church alone and its liturgical action but a problem of contemporary life.

A third problem resulting from the efforts at reform was a loss of the liturgical community. The present age is a highly individualistic one. This aspect of contemporary society, like the others I have mentioned, has its effect on the liturgy. There is no doubt that the leaders of the liturgical movement and those who developed the imagery of the Mystical Body emphasized and acted on a conviction that the formation of a community of worshippers was a key element. They did so based upon theological and especially historical principles, and were successful in a limited way. But in a world where the emphasis is not on a continuity with the past or a historical understanding but on a pressing forward to the future, it is extremely difficult to create and maintain community.

GPS: Of course, this is the hazard of any kind of reform, isn't it? It calls past practices and ideas into question, and forms new ways of speaking and acting. Yet, such an activity should not be confused with a general repudiation of the past, a refusal to learn from it or to recognize its power in forming us.

AM: The community receives its symbols from the past. They come to us laden with meaning because of their place in the long history of the community that we might have just lately joined. To enter that community requires an education whereby I come to know those symbols and make them my own. I have mentioned before the need for a careful catechesis. In our age, this is often set aside in favour of "spontaneity," another demand of our age that works against both of the essential characteristics of good liturgy we are speaking of at the moment, namely its historical and communal natures.

An emphasis on spontaneity breaks up the community. It becomes difficult, then, to harmonize and unify an already divergent group in and through the symbols of the liturgy, since those very symbols are called into question. Moreover, it is difficult for this particular group to express itself as part of the long, historical tradition, if the emphasis is on the immediate self-expression, on the satisfaction of individual needs by whatever means seems appropriate to the individual at that moment. That is not to say that spontaneity should be totally lacking from the liturgy, but it cannot reduce the congregation to a mere group of persons acting individually. The action of the liturgy requires acceptance and agreement of the community, past and present. This continuity is what makes the action of this particular community in Africa or Asia or North America the liturgical action of the whole Christian community.

GPS: To summarize then, I understand you to be saying that the liturgy must not only express the belief of the community but also form the belief of each individual. If the liturgy were only to teach and form the community, then it could become hollow, empty; if it were only to express what I happen to feel at the moment, then it would ultimately lose its essential character as historical, communal and symbolic.

AM: Associated with this problem is what might be called the crisis of authority in both the Church and the world. In worship, it is seen in the attitude of those who ask, "Why should I be told how to pray, to use just this text, to perform just these actions prescribed by an 'authority'?" This attitude was clearly evident after the Council, when individuals and groups thought that each liturgy should be created anew, without reference to anything other than the immediate needs and feelings of those to be involved. Such constant, creative efforts demand a lot of energy and ingenuity. Eventually they became very tedious and time consuming, and increasingly bizarre in order to provide ever-newer ways to celebrate.

GPS: It might be helpful to recall what any fine musician or dancer would say about the apparent ease with a great performance is given —that such ease is entirely apparent. Hours of practice, of research and study, of careful planning, make possible the exciting and creative moments.

AM: I recall the comment of Clarence Rivers, the liturgical musician known for his lively music. He was asked how he was able to be so spontaneous, and his reply was, "I practise a lot."

Let me repeat, spontaneity in some measure is essential to good liturgy, but it must be held in tension with the historical and communal nature of celebration. That is one of the primary functions of authority: to provide unity and a structure where the spontaneous can occur. This is particularly important given the rise of small Christian communities as the most common way people gather to worship. The danger is that these small groups develop idiosyncratic liturgies that cause them to lose contact with the universal Church. In a way, the liturgy itself is a vehicle for creating the unity of the Church.

All these various problems I have mentioned, especially as they are conditioned by contemporary culture, will remain with us for some time. Efforts to deal with them will require several decades.

GPS: As well, perhaps we should remember that these problems are encountered primarily in Western culture, though not exclusively so. If we were speaking outside of North America, for example, our concerns would be somewhat different.

To move to another topic now—could you speak from your experience of Canada about the state of the liturgy here, its problems and its successes?

AM: Certainly. First, despite Canada's size and complexity, there is not a great diversity of application. Of course, some dioceses are more conservative, and others are more open. That depends partly upon the leadership: how the bishop and priests are able to open up the treasury of the liturgy to the faithful and enlist their help to do more than merely implement the letter of the law.

The success of the liturgical renewal depends upon the degree of liturgical spirituality that can be fostered in the local communities. In Canada, we have barely begun to prepare people to engage in worship with all that such a spirituality implies. I do not mean simply the ability to organize things well. It is not a matter of efficiency or "crowd control." Parish liturgical committees will be successful only if they are well-formed in the historical, theological and pastoral principles of the liturgy, and if they can radiate this deeper understanding and sense of the liturgy to the rest of the parish. The activity of a few will attract others to the celebration and help them to discover the sacred, to appreciate the symbols, to experience the sense of community that the liturgy can provide.

In this sense, the faithful will not learn from books. They will learn from being led into and by engaging in authentic worship with those who are themselves deeply committed to its inherent principles and values. The education takes place by osmosis, and certainly in the context of a prayerful life. Day by day, season by season, we begin to notice that the liturgy is and how it accomplishes its purposes.

That is not to say that serious research and study are not also part of what must be done to further the work of renewal. In anthropology, the nature of human symbolism is being increasingly investigated; such research must be brought to bear on the theology of the liturgy. Both psychology and sociology, the two sciences most in conversation with theology, must also be consulted for what they can teach us about the nature of celebration, about the formation of communities, about the dynamics of individual and group participation. In theological studies, developments are taking place in sacramental theology. In the comparative study of liturgies, the richness of the Eastern Church is being brought to bear on the theory and practice of the West. Finally, ecumenical studies contribute significantly to the convergence of liturgical practice. In turn, this convergence, for example, in the sacrament of initiation, helps to bring about a new common theological understanding among the Christian Churches. The liturgy is helping to push forward the ecumenical movement.

The area of theology that provides the greatest difficulty at the moment is ecclesiology. One may believe in God and in Christ but have problems accepting the Church. Since the liturgy is the prayer and worship of the Church, if I do not like the Church, if I am not at home in it, why should I conform to and participate in the Church's worship? That would be one extreme.

There are conflicting models of the Church at work within the living Church. Let me give an example of the effect this has. For some people the primary work of the Church is social action; for them elaborate services in grand cathedrals are unacceptable and unnecessary in face of the millions of poor and starving in the world. Opposed to this view might be a sacramentalist notion that the celebration of the liturgy is all that need be done, and the power of God will take care of the rest.

Obviously, the truth of such tensions is that neither position is the whole truth. If liturgy remains isolated from life, it is not true to its own inner nature. It must issue in social concern, in ministry in the world.

It is interesting to note that in the history of the liturgical movement in this century, the establishment of liturgical centres with vigorous renewal was always followed by the establishment of centres for social action. For example, Collegeville in Minnesota began as a liturgical centre, and its leader Virgil Michael subsequently became a leader in social action. Similarly, the Oxford Movement, which was clearly a liturgical and sacramental movement, issued in social action in the slums of England.

Another tension involving how we understand the Church centres on the connection of the local with the universal Church. The communion that makes up the Church is a unity in diversity, but just how much diversity is possible is the question. How unique can any one group be without losing its connection with all the others?

Yet another form of this tension is the relation between apostolicity and catholicity. If I want to be true to the apostolic and orthodox faith, doctrine, way of life, and liturgy, I must question the degree to which I can adapt to the contemporary and local situation. On the other hand, I cannot abandon the need for catholicity for an ability to adapt to the great variety of situations of both locale and culture in which Christian life expresses itself. The terms "enculturation" and "provincialism" express the ideal and the danger, respectively.

In all these matters, it is the larger question that is not only a matter of the liturgy but of doctrine and moral principles as well: what can and must change, and what must remain permanent?

GPS: That would seem to be the case particularly in situations where the liturgy is made the work of a small group as opposed to a large parish, which by its nature forces one to deal with catholicity. In a small group, there may be authenticity to itself and its members but not to the Church at large and to its apostolic traditions.

AM: It is interesting at this point to quote the remarks of Martin Luther, as a liturgical reformer:

> My faith requires spontaneity in its expression; but charity requires structures so everyone can find a place in the community of worshippers. That requires a certain tempering of my spontaneity.

I might mention at this point a matter of much controversy—the use of the liturgy for political purposes. My general principle is that the liturgy should not be politicized. Now, the liturgy is not apolitical, in the sense that it does not have anything to do with real life or that it does not reflect the political climate of a particular locale, along with every other aspect of human life. However, I would urge that the liturgy be not *used* for the sake of partisan political ends. Liturgical action is to be a time of unity in which all that divides us, whether it be race, social situation, political affiliations and so on, is set aside by the fundamental unity that we all share as Christians because of our Baptism.

GPS: Perhaps we could say that the work of the liturgy as the critic of human existence does not result in the same kind of criticism that politics and political parties undertake. It has its own unique form and content.

The danger is the same in the interpretation of the Scriptures: do I turn them into something else in order to make them relevant for the present, or do I treat them as having a unique purpose and message?

AM: Yes, when I preach I must preach the love of God and neighbour in accordance with the texts. Can we systematically exclude certain people from the liturgy because we see them as not belonging for one reason or another? Is the liturgy not the very place where diverse groups are confronted with the radical unity that binds them together, where they must face the task of settling their differences, of finding solutions to what it is that keeps them apart?

GPS: It would seem that the situation is quite different when one compares, for example, Poland with certain South American countries. In a country where the opposition is between believers and non-believers, it is difficult to resolve the tensions *within* the Church, because the non-believers are not part of the liturgical action and life of the Church. In countries where the Church is made up of members from many social classes, the challenge is to accord all members their place in the liturgy without, of course, failing to preach the Gospel message that we are all sinners and that we are all unjust to one another in many very real ways. To give an example of a delicate matter experienced especially here in North America, the role of women in the Church has some similarities.

AM: Exactly. The liturgy should not so much express the injustice and division but rather the unity and harmony of the Church, despite its problems.

GPS: Could we say then that the liturgy can have a role of education in these matters?

AM: Yes, every true Christian doctrine ought to have its manifestation somehow in the liturgy. Historically, the liturgy was always a source of education for the faithful in the doctrines and practices of the Church. It provides a way for these things to be gradually assimilated.

GPS: It strikes me that, in keeping with your opening remarks about how the document on the liturgy as the first fruit of the Council was itself a result of the grass-roots work of the Church, so many of the topics we have just discussed are proof that the liturgy remains the place where development of the Church is reflected and fostered.

AM: I think there must be a real effort on all levels in the Church, from the hierarchy to the parish level, to form groups of people who will seriously engage in discussion and form small liturgical communities as a leaven in the Church for the development of true liturgical spirituality. They will gradually attract others who will see in these groups the effects of study and action for the sake of adopting a liturgical spirituality such as the Council suggests to us. Others will see in such people just how engagement in the liturgical life of the Church can transform all of life. It will not happen, of course, without a sincere, deep and affectionate love of the Church. That is not easy to achieve. Perhaps the more one enters into the liturgical life of the Church, the more one will come to know and love the Church.

GPS: Thank you for your comments. I know they come not only from many years of study and teaching but also from a great deal of practical experience of the liturgy.

COMMENTARY ON THE

Decree on the Instruments of Social Communication

Inter Mirifica

DAVID ELEY

It is twenty years since the Second Vatican Council, when more than two thousand bishops sat in the main aisle of St. Peter's, surrounded by theological experts and observers from other Churches and religions. This anniversary is a good time to examine the importance of this ecclesiastical event. The attention of this paper is on the *Decree on the Instruments of Social Communication, Inter Mirifica*,[1] by most accounts one of the minor documents of the Council. The major documents that express more centrally the spirit of the Council are the *Dogmatic Constitution on the Church, Dogmatic Constitution on Divine Revelation, Constitution on the Sacred Liturgy* and *Pastoral Constitution on the Church in the Modern World*.

The Council was clearly a big event in the life of the Church, but was it as important for the rest of the world? Since it probably has had little or no impact on several areas of the world, we should not think of it in global terms. Attitudes about the effectiveness of the Council have ranged widely—from the view that the Council was the end of an old era and the dawn of a new age, to the view that the Council's attachment to old doctrine and patterns of thought had moved the Church perhaps from the thirteenth to the seventeenth century, but that it had not yet faced the realities of the culture and sciences of the last two hundred years. For example, it is helpful that the Council changed the liturgy from the Latin to the vernacular; but this is not such a striking event, since other Christian Churches did the same four hundred years ago.

Inter Mirifica is of interest for several reasons. It can be considered as a first application of what the Council was preoccupied with—the Church's role in the modern world. It expresses its concerns for the activities of the modern world, but it sets them in a frame of thought that does not do them justice. To balance this, however, it must be added immediately that, in the document The *Pastoral Constitution on the Church in the Modern World, Gaudium et Spes*,[2] written several years later,[3] there are several passages on culture and communications that do reflect a renewed identity for the Church and a deep respect for human society. This is strong evidence that two years of Council experience did reframe those ideas.

Second, *Inter Mirifica* is interesting because the press, cinema, radio and television, when placed in the Church's history, are relatively new experiences; the Church's reaction to them is telling because there is not a two-thousand-year theological tradition to go back to. If the topic were faith and justification or the sacraments, surely references would have to be made to the Council of Trent, since these themes were major preoccupations during the Reformation. While there is some parallel between the use of modern media and the use in past cultures of art, manuscripts and stained-glass windows, it is the rapid transmission of information, news, public opinion and mass entertainment that distinguishes the modern media. There is, therefore, an opportunity here for a more original reflection than on those topics that must go back to the origins of the Christian age and whose language is weighted with the theological traditions and philosophical assumptions of Augustine or Thomas, for example. These theological traditions cannot be applied in the same way when you are talking about the daily newspaper.[4]

To the Council's credit, the Church is preoccupied with this issue of contemporary communications to some extent, and has produced a document on the instruments of communications, "those [inventions] which by their very nature can reach and influence not only individual men, but the masses themselves, even the whole of society." The Council Fathers could have but did not choose to write about other aspects of the modern world (hydro plants or automotive factories, for example). They knew that the media of communication are at least an ideological issue: "But the Church is also aware that men can employ these gifts against the mind of the divine Benefactor, and abuse them to their own undoing." There is perhaps some recognition of a threat; the media, as others have claimed more recently,[5] are the religion of the secular culture, with their own mythology, rituals and worship like the Church. The attention that the Council gives to such a topic is of some interest to those whose religion is that of Abraham, Isaac, Jacob and Jesus and whose commitment is to the development of their societies.

PRE-COUNCIL

The communications media changed radically after the turn of the century.[6] By the 1920's, the press and radio were prolific. The American cinema, with directors and actors like D. W. Griffith and

Charlie Chaplin, had begun to create a world-wide audience. Most European countries were also starting to produce their own films, and in Russia, film in the hands of Eisenstein and Pudovkin was serving the revolution. The Church's first significant reaction was in 1928 when the Office catholique internationale du cinéma (O.C.I.C.) was created. It rewarded good films with prizes, and presented warnings and ratings from a Catholic point of view to guide audiences.

On June 29, 1936, Pope Pius XI wrote the letter *Vigilanti Cura,* on the subject of the cinema. This was the first time that any Pope had addressed in a central way the question of the mass media.[7] It is a fairly forward-looking letter consistent with his own social teaching as expressed in *Quadragesimo Anno* (1931) and Leo XIII's *Rerum Novarum* (1891). These important documents not only dealt with "the conditions of the worker" but serve as a "social charter in the broadest sense," treating topics of the technological world, the working class, ownership of property and capital. It is in this social context that it expresses its concern for modern culture. The encyclical praises the efforts of the Legion of Decency and encourages the bishops, the film producers in every country and especially the consumers to be aware of the human and moral dimensions of the cinema. It makes some practical and administrative recommendations. This important document became the foundation for the official Church practice of the next twenty years. Throughout his papacy, Pius XII made seventeen personal statements about the cinema; the O.C.I.C. made twenty-nine others.

In 1955, the pope twice gave an address called "The Ideal Film" to cinematographers and film producers in Italy, in which he spoke with great interest and enthusiasm about the influence of the cinema in a technological civilization. He concerned himself with the myths, the personalities, the spectators and the economic implications of film. He was aware of the quasi-magical, dream-like quality of the cinema, and indicated certain potential difficulties in the film industry between the artistic and the technical dimensions. Reflecting the psychological preoccupations of the 1950's, he expressed concern for the power of the unconscious and the subconscious in the images and themes. But basically, this was a humanistic document, proclaiming that the values of the cinema should be the values of the whole human person. At the annual meeting of the O.C.I.C. in Havana, 1957, the concluding statements summed up the papal opinion in the following way:

> The cinema is in the modern world a privileged instrument, but providentially at man's disposition, to make it comply with a specific and authentic culture, where in effect, regarding the instructional, aesthetic, moral and spiritual value of the images and themes, the cinema provides man an opening to the world and to the realities which work to enhance mankind

and contribute to a reconciliation and an understanding among individuals, classes, nations and races.[8]

On September 8, 1957, Pius XII wrote a letter, *Miranda Prorsus*, on the means of communication, cinema, radio, television and the press. This is the first statement on communication in the larger sense, not just on the cinema or the radio but on a variety of media that shape modern culture. This too was a generally enthusiastic letter. It had a first careless rapture quality in its expression of wonder at the powers of modern communication. This is perhaps the same tone that prevailed at the famous meeting between Pius XI and Marconi during which the pope invited Marconi to establish Vatican Radio.

Just before the Council, John XXIII wrote two important letters, *Pacem in Terris* and *Mater et Magistra*. Although they do not speak of the technology of communication directly, they do comment on the Church's attitude to the contemporary world. The new spirit was to be one of openness and aggiornamento, bringing-up-to-date. At the same time, in his apostolic constitution, *Humanae Salutis*, with which he convoked the Council officially on December 25, 1961, the pope made the link between the technological world and atheism:

> It is a question in fact of bringing the modern world into contact with the vivifying and perennial energies of the gospel, a world which exalts itself with its conquests in the technical and scientific fields, but which brings also the consequences of a temporal order which some have wished to reorganize excluding God.[9]

John XXIII's spirit was one of enquiry and dialogue. He wanted to engage the Church in the conversation with the world.

THE COUNCIL: PREPARATION OF THE TEXT

As was the case for most of the Council's work, a committee was established to begin the documentary work even before the official announcement of the Council.[10] The Segretariato della stampa e dello spettacolo, the Secretariat for the Press and the Cinema, was established on June 5, 1960, as one of ten commissions and two secretariats to work for the preparation period 1960–1962. Archbishop Martin John O'Connor, rector of the North American College and the president of the Pontifical Commission on Film, Radio and Television, was appointed president of the secretariat. The members included Bishop George A. Beck of Salford, U.K., Monsignor James Tuceck of the Roman Press Office of the National Catholic Welfare Conference, Father A. Andrews, O.F.M., and Monsignor A.M. Deskur as secretary. This group worked in three sections: the press, the cinema and radio/

television. They drew up an Index Argumentorum, which was approved and subsequently used as the basis of a draft text sent to the Council Fathers in August 1962. This draft proposed the following schema:

Introduction:
I   Church's Doctrine
     i   Teaching of the Church
     ii Defending the objective moral order
     iii The duties of citizens and civil authorities
II   How the Church does her work, the Apostolate
     i   Spreading truth and Christian doctrine
     ii Aids to spreading truth
III Church discipline and order
     i   Church discipline
     ii The organs of Church authority
IV Some observations on certain media of social communication
     i   The press
     ii Cinema
     iii Radio and television
     iv Other media

This document was laid before the Council on November 21, 1962, and was brought up for discussion two days later. The reason it was introduced at this time, it is speculated by Karlheinz Schmidthüs, is that it was considered an "easier" schema and the Council needed a change of pace after the exhausting sessions on the liturgy and some of the debate on Revelation. Since it was near the end of the original list, few Fathers would have done any preparation for it. Cardinal Certo, president of the commission responsible for presenting it, said so fairly boldly. It was of undoubted pastoral importance but the subject was not theological. He asked that it be passed without a great deal of debate.

To establish the pastoral urgency, Archbishop Stourm of Sens provided the statistics for the prodigious phenomena of the mass media: 8000 daily newspapers with a daily circulation of 300 million; 22,000 periodicals with a circulation of 200 million; 2500 films annually with an audience of 17,000 million; 600 broadcast stations with an audience of 400 million and 1000 television stations with an audience of 120 million. Archbishop D'Souza of Nagpur and Cardinal Léger of Montréal commented that the draft document unduly stressed the rights of the Church to own and use the media; it was more important for the Council to vindicate the rights of all people to know the truth. Cardinal Wyszynski of Poland echoed this opinion when he said that the Church should not concentrate on itself but show instead more interest in the aspirations of the wider human culture. Two specific objections were also voiced: that the document did not acknowledge adequately the role of the laity in the press and other media of communication; and that it was inappropriate for the Council to make any declaration at all because this issue was not of universal theological importance. Some recommended that the Council's statement should be put in a papal paraconciliar document so as not to have the authority of a conciliar text, which should be reserved for important and central themes like the liturgy and Revelation.

After two and one half days, Cardinal Tisserant closed the debate. The document was approved in substance, with the proviso that it be drastically pruned and include the basic doctrinal and pastoral directives recapitulated. The work was duly undertaken and the text revised.

According to Schmidthüs, the Council turned to the *Decree on the Instruments of Social Communication* in the second session so the work of the Council not seem so meagre. Although much time had been spent on the constitution on the liturgy, there were not many other major works to show. This document was distributed on November 11, 1963; it was introduced three days later at the sixty-seventh general congregation by Archbishop Stourm. The original 40 pages had been cut to 9, the 114 paragraphs down to 24.

The text has two chapters, the first dealing with the teaching of the Church, the second with the pastoral activity of the Church concerning the instruments of social communication. An introduction announces the concerns of the human spirit, in the context of a schedule, that is, the culture's need for refreshment and refinement, and a vigilance against moral abuse. The text concludes with an injunction that an instruction be drawn up later by experts, and with an entreaty that "men of good will, especially those who control these instruments," strive to use them for the good of mankind. A note is added that, as ancient artistic achievements glorified the name of the Lord, so might modern inventions. The teaching section begins with the assertion of the Church's right to use and possess the instruments of communications (3); with expressions of concern for morality, particularly because of the "unconscious influences" of the media (4); and with an affirmation of a society's right to be informed, in truth, justice and decency (5). It discusses public opinion, its importance and the power of forming it, and encourages each person to form worthy views (8). Then it enunciates the duties of diverse groups, of users, of young people, of professionals and finally of civil authorities (9–12). The second chapter explores ways the Church might strive to use the instruments apostolically, for example, pastors in their preaching (13) and the Catholic press (14). It encourages the training of people working in communications (15) and audiences (16). And it offers directions on how this ministry might be financed (17–18) and institutionalized in national (21) and international (22) offices.

There were four additions beyond the original text: on lay co-operation (13–19); on the protection of youth (10–12); on the faithful's support of the Catholic press (14); and on the theatre (14). While the majority of bishops favoured the document, two somewhat significant critical reactions were registered against the decree at this stage. One came from a group of American journalists covering the Council. John Cogley from *Commonweal*, Robert Kaiser of *Time* and *Life*, and Michael Novak from the *New Republic* joined three theologians working for the Council, John Courtney Murray, S.J. (American), Jean Danièlou, S.J. (French) and Jorge Meija (Argentinian). They called the document retrograde and criticized the text for its moralistic approach and lack of respect for the integrity of art. They asked about the originators of information in a society and their obligations: the text focussed mainly on the carriers of information. They questioned the implications for secrecy and the authority of the government if all the opinions of the document were taken at face value. They also believed that the document implied that the Catholic press had a quasi-infallible doctrinal authority, as if the secular press contributed nothing to the formation of public opinion in the Church. Finally, they were upset that ecclesiastical authority could be somehow put between journalists and their employers.

The second reaction was more important and perhaps one of the most interesting in the Council. Ninety bishops of the Council also wrote a document opposing the official text. The day before the vote, these bishops, led by Cardinals Frings and Alfrink, handed out their text on the steps of St. Peter's. The publishing of these handbills caused some heated words at the Council and the president, Cardinal Tisserant, publicly reprimanded Archbishop Felici. The substance of the petition was that the document speaks of the rights of the Church but disregards the fact that all communication springs from the search for truth and the desire to express it. They questioned the understanding of the nature of the media. Social communication is not just a technical instrument but a human dialogue, a social process, important in education and other human affairs. The text's oversight of the contribution of lay people suggests a distorted view of the Church itself. Other bishops believed that a general decision on the question of the media was not possible because the media themselves were so intimately tied up with national and regional concerns. Rather, the media should be a topic for an episcopal conference. This approach would serve collegiality.

These tactics had some effect. But still, most Council Fathers were satisfied with the scope of the text and considered it a sufficient if small step forward. The initial vote[11] on November 14 had about 100 opponents. Four days later, there were 503 negative voices on the second ballot;[12] one-quarter of the Council Fathers were opposed. Some wanted the document to be withdrawn completely but there were no procedures for this. At the time of the formal final vote on December 4, 1963, 1960 voted for, 164 against and 27 abstained.

The document had been caught in a crossfire between two groups: the first said the topic was not up to the level of an Ecumenical Council and should not have been treated in the first place; the second said the document needed a renewed pastoral view, the kind reflected in several other documents of the Council, and it was too important to be rushed through quickly.

THE TEXT

The *Decree on the Instruments of Social Communication* is divided into four parts: the introduction (1–2); on the teaching of the Church (3–12); on pastoral activity (13–22); and the conclusion (23–24). The language is terse, without a strong developed line of thought. Rather, it has many short statements on separate topics. The introduction is the most expansive in its use of language, in contrast with the conclusion, which seems ritualized and perfunctory. Where it speaks of the technology "which bears on the human spirit" and "for the refreshment and refinement of the spirit," the introduction echoes the enthusiasm of the letters of earlier popes. But the tone quickly changes when it notes the vigilance and moral directives required to deal with the abuses, damages and perversities.

The teaching section is preoccupied with morality rather than the religious relationship of each person with God in a contemporary culture. Even the comments about art warn of moral evils and assert that the moral order is higher than the artistic. It addresses the duties of the users, particularly the young, of the professionals and of the civil authorities. One paragraph on public opinion deserves particular attention (8). Here the document encourages each person to form and to voice worthy views on public affairs. It repeats the concept of "the public" used by Pius XII; it ought to be explored to uncover the meaning of "the public" and "the public domain" in a modern state and in the Church. It is of some credit to the Council Fathers that the document deals with the question so favourably.

The pastoral section is concerned with the apostolic use of the instruments of the communications media and the training necessary for an extensive use of these. The spoken and underlying assumption here is that Church members, both clerical and lay, should use the media as much as possible for the work of the Church. Users, critics and audiences should be educated for this extensive evangelization through the media. Money should be gathered through national annual collections and the bishops should establish administrative structures in each nation and internationally as well. A clerical tone permeates much of this, especially article 13. The document encourages pastors to fulfil their duties speedily to preach with the new media and lay persons to "lend direct aid." We can accept the directive that "religious shepherds" should be involved with their "normal preaching responsibilities," but to relegate the lay involvement to an ancillary role is inadmissible given the Church's lack of involvement in media activities and the extensive professional experience of lay Catholics.

What is an appropriate starting point for the question of the Church's use of media? The Church is entitled to "own and use media" (1) but its experience in different parts of the world shows this possession depends on the acceptance of other basic freedoms. People have the right to know the truth. From this right flows the freedom of the press, which has financial, technical, organizational, intellectual and cultural components. It might have been a better starting point to affirm the freedom of the press rather than the Church's right of possession. Perhaps at the bottom of this is the question, does the Church consider itself a complete society or a part of human society? *Pacem in Terris* had termed the right to information as a natural right of man (12). Public and private information, with the constraints of accuracy and completeness as it is collected and diffused, is the basis of public opinion and a free press. And public opinion is the "rightful heritage of a normal society," Pius XII had written in *Miranda Prorsus* (1957). The Council itself was a good example of openness to the press and to the rights of human society. This same troublesome tone reappears in article 12, in the discussion of the responsibilities of the state for upholding minimal social standards. Such a position—that these instruments are subordinate to the common good—could be used to justify many forms of undue censorship.

The section on the press (14) expressed very high expectations for the Catholic media. It seems to present as the ideal a Christian judgment about everything that happens formed in "harmony with natural law and with Catholic teachings and precepts." Again, it is difficult to know how the Catholic media would have any greater access to the truth than their secular counterparts. Here is a little glimpse of a pre-Vatican II description of a Christian—a person enlightened by natural law and Catholic teachings, who can see the truth. Vatican II encouraged us to share our search for the truth with men and women of diverse religious commitments. What is needed in this section and throughout is a theology of communication that might address the nature of the media and the character of human dialogue,[13] a consistent interpretation of culture and the Gospel behind the text.

It is interesting to note some of the initial external reactions to the document. The text is isolated from many of the other documents and concerns of the Council with which the subject matter has direct affinity. For example, it does not mention any connections with Revelation or with ecumenism. What more fitting place to speak of the power of the Word of God and of our relationships with others with whom we share our countries and this world? The context of the decree is the institution of the Church, and not even a renewed view of the Church at that.

Whom does *Inter Mirifica* serve? Not the concerns of professional journalists, experts in the field, or the people at large, as the plea circulated on the steps of St. Peter's stated. As a community that speaks publicly of God and is the keeper of sacred texts, the Church should have a more developed view of the salvific aspects of communication and at least struggle to understand this in the context of the contemporary cultures.[14] If Christ brings redemption, talk about Christ can be redemptive. The point is not to control the mass media but to encourage a creative and constructive development within the institutions of the media. Instead of forcing the media within a predefined system of thought, the goal should be to help release the media and modern culture from their bonds.

Finally, the most devastating criticism that can be brought against this document and many other expressions of the Council is that they overlook the realities of the Church behind the Iron Curtain and in the Third World. Many of the Council Fathers knew well that the conditions of Christian life in the Soviet Bloc are radically different from the West and that the place for growth and vitality of Catholicism and Christianity was in the Third World, most often under conditions of economic exploitation and socially unjust structures. It was already too late to talk of fine tuning the European and North American middle-class Christianity. This document on communications might have expressed some of the experience of these new Churches, but there is not a word about this. As well, the international media have a vital role in the development of people, culture and Church throughout the whole world.

Although the decree on communication can be judged to be seriously deficient, other documents of the Council do address some of the substantive material missing here. For example, the *Pastoral Constitution on the Church in the Modern World, Gaudium et Spes*, has several pertinent sections. In the passage on the community of mankind (GS 23), the document speaks of modern technical advances and their relationship to technical progress and, at the deeper level, to interpersonal relationships. Later, the text pays particular attention to five problems of special urgency: fostering nobility of the family and marriage; the proper development of culture; economic and social life; the life of the political community; and fostering peace and promotion of a community of nations. This second section (GS 53–62) deals with the development of cultures in the new age. It describes this as an age with a critical judgment helped along by the exact sciences, with a psychological explanation of human activities, with an appreciation of change in history. This is an age bearing the influence of industrialization, urbanization and mass culture, having more leisure and moving to a more universal human culture. The section concludes with the announcement of the birth of a new humanism characterized by freedom of inquiry and expression: "In order that such persons may fulfil their proper function, let it be recognized that all the faithful, clerical and lay, possess a lawful freedom of inquiry and of thought, and the freedom to express their minds humbly and courageously about those matters in which they enjoy competence" (GS 62). Such attitudes and ideas could have made the difference if they had been applied to the *Decree on the Instruments of Social Communication*.

POST-CONCILIAR

The decree recommends that a pastoral instruction be drawn up so that "all the principles and norms enunciated by this Council concerning the instruments of social communication may achieve their effect" (23). In June 1971, the Pontifical Commission for the Media of Social Communication published the document *Communications: A Pastoral Instruction on the Media, Public Opinion and Human Progress (Communio et Progressio).*[15] This document makes up for many of the faults of *Inter Mirifica*. It was written with the whole Council in mind and with the benefit of the rather harsh criticism that the decree occasioned. It states from the outset that the chief aim of social communication is "the unity and advancement of men living in society." It places itself in the context of the major documents of Vatican II.

Considerably longer than *Inter Mirifica*, it presents a more balanced view with approving expressions on the "great roundtable" and the partnership in the business of the human race (19), and on such critical questions as the concentration of power, mental idleness and passivity, and the incessant appeal to the emotions.[16] It sees communication both as an act of co-operation in the divine work of creation and consecrations (7) and the way people become partners in the business of the human race (19).

In 1974, a synod of the United States National Conference of Catholic Bishops took as its theme "The Use of Modern Means of Communication as Instruments of Evangelization." A year later, in his letter *Evangelii Nutiandi*, Pope Paul VI integrated these same concerns into his theme: "The Church would feel guilty before the Lord if she did not utilize these powerful means." He also touched on one of the ambiguous assumptions, the dual desire to reach vast numbers of people and yet do so in a way that touches "each individually...as though he were the only person being addressed." Here is one of the crucial problems with the Church's involvement with the media: the allurement of the mass audience on the one hand and the knowledge on the other that the Christ of God is a person and is probably best communicated in a more intimate way.

Nonetheless, the ideas and the direction of the Council have been developed and continued in important ways since then. For Communication Sunday, the Pontifical Commission publishes an annual statement which has developed a different dimension of the communication ministry of the Church each year. (The subject of these letters would make an interesting historical study that is outside the scope of this paper.) Despite a consistency of effort at many levels within the Church, the use of media remains difficult and elusive for the Church.

After twenty years, both the practice and the theology of communications are still sorely underdeveloped. The practice of communications, radio and television, for example, has not progressed much since an interesting beginning in the 1950's with Bishop Fulton J. Sheen. There are many more programs but they are not creating significant regular audiences, with the exception of the television evangelists. But some special religious programs have attracted large audiences, for example, theatrical films like Franco Zefirelli's *Jesus of Nazareth* broadcast during Holy Week, and the extensively covered papal visits.

QUESTIONS FOR TODAY IN CANADA

The final section of this paper will take up several questions that are implied by the decree of Vatican II or at least are suggested by the reflection we have had in the twenty-year interval. Some have been partially answered; others have been left untouched.

The technology and practice of communications throughout most of the world have not stood still during these last twenty years. It is an energetic industry that has been independent for the main part from the opinions or practices of the Church. Many of the issues today would be the same even without this decree on the instruments of social communication.

How does the Christian community live in a modern culture that uses the electronic means of communication? To reduce a complex issue to black and white terms for the purposes of clarity: Are these communication channels fundamental instruments for the proclamation of the Kingdom of God and therefore to be embraced? Or does the Christian individually or collectively need a retreat from this market-place of manipulative messages to find the Kingdom elsewhere? The choice is between the model of the catacomb Church of the first two centuries in hostile Rome (Christ against culture) or the model of the medieval village around its monastery or cathedral (Christ the centre of culture). There is a need for a theology of technology or at least of technological culture. Even the title of the decree suggests an instrumental view of technology, a technology to be used. The document did not embrace a more interactional view of communication—communication as a form of communion, as a foundation of community, the way we are going to live together in this world with people of non-Christian traditions and with people of no belief. The decision expressed in the document to get involved with media use is attuned to the aggiornamento the Church longs to experience. More deliberation is needed, however, to avoid being naive about the complexities of modern culture.

In what sense is the Church still a sanctuary, a holy place where we can find God away from the market-place of competing images and the Babylon of contradictory messages? Although offering sanctuary is one function of the Church, it is not possible to cut the Church off from culture. The Church itself needs information, publication and proclamation to sustain the ordinary activities of Christian communities. Catholic literature is very important for some. And the works of secular writers like Mary Gordon, Walker Percy, Flannery O'Connor and John Updike show us how writers with a spiritual vision deal with the culture in which we live. Films by Bresson or Bergman, for example, serve in the same way, to provide insights into our existence, our suffering and the action of grace.

Will the Church apply its ideas about openness to itself? The Council was very well covered by the most of the world's press, including the global broadcast by satellite of Pope John XXIII's opening of the first session of the Council.

This is not to suggest that the relationship between the press and the Church should be the same as that with the state. But surely, freedom of information and open discussion should be hallmarks of the religious press.

Is it possible to proclaim the Gospel of Christ to vast audiences world-wide or at least nationally, and at the same time, address an individual in a personal way? This is a significant contradiction. Mass media mean mass audiences. Is it even desirable to have a mass Christian culture or must the Church necessarily be enculturated in a great diversity of communities? Television, after all, is often impersonal, providing at best only a distraction. Further, it creates an illusion of personal contact with the audience. Mass culture is certainly not the parish and liturgical life that has been the basis of Christian community for several centuries. This is the unresolved issue for most religious television, particularly the evangelical variety.

Do the advice and opinions expressed in the decree apply to the Third

World countries or are they written from and for a Western perspective? As in other areas of life in the Third World, there is a growing dependency on the industrialized countries for media productions, both informational and cultural. The media are owned by very few people but used by the many who are often disenfranchised. Mass media do not comprise a dialogue.

This is true in Canada, but in the Third World the situation is more critical. On the one hand, it is too expensive for a small developing country to produce its own news and cultural programs; on the other, the growth of local and national cultural identities is threatened or impossible when all the media come from the dominant world powers. More importantly, many African countries have become the ideological battlefields between the European democracies and the Soviets.

Should church members be encouraged to take part in religious broadcasting on the radio? For example, would it be appropriate in the Canadian North to produce Christian programs for the Innuit, many of whom are not Christians? The social context for all media messages is of the utmost moral concern. The Church at the Council implied that it no longer considers itself the spiritual centre of the world. Much of the real dynamism, spiritually speaking, is in the Third World and among people who live in structurally unjust conditions. The questions of social peace in the Third World is connected to a critique of unjust and exploitative media systems.

Does the Church have some more specific reflection or teaching for those Christians living in the Soviet Bloc, a major part of humanity? The political and public conditions of life there are considerably different from developed technological democracies.

Should the Church speak only with an official voice? Surely being catholic means a diversity that at the level of expression would mean many different voices? When the bishops in Canada spoke as a minority in their economic and ethical statement, they faced heated criticism. They admitted that they might be wrong on detailed economic theories, but at the level of human concern they were not. This is a hopeful sign, and a sign of Christian humility.

CONCLUSIONS

When we assess the importance of a document written twenty years ago, we must take into account our own experience with the Church. For example, such disappointments as our Church's not getting involved with other Churches in a multi-faith satellite television service in Canada colour my view of how capable we are of living as Church in a contemporary Canadian culture.

Although the Church through the Council encouraged its members to be active in the media, the results have been less than expected: little participation and not much influence on the media. Either very few seem to be listening or the Church has not grasped its situation very well and has been sending confusing messages to its members. We may fear the manipulative power of the media; nonetheless, it is possible to hope that deeply human and respectful uses can be made of the media. We can take more than an artistic and literary interest in these products; there is also a political and social argument involved here. The possibility of renewed religious culture in this form of communicative social action is what is most interesting to the Church.

On the other hand, serious and unanswered questions remain about the nature of religion and spectacle. Much of what the mass media provide is spectacle, something to be looked at without making any personal commitment or becoming involved. Does great spectacle even have anything to do with religion? Participatory worship in liturgy, for example, has never been conceived of as spectacle. Nor is it evident in the life of Jesus or the lives of the saints. One of Jesus' temptations in the desert was to acquire all the kingdoms of the earth, which could be interpreted as a form of popularity and grandeur in exchange for false worship.

What is the nature, then, of the religious dimension in a communicative event, if it is not spectacle? It is probably something intrinsic in the language and narratives of transformation, and the representation of self-sacrifice, for example. Through these explorations the media do open up some possibilities for the Christian community but not in propagandistic or spectacular ways.

At the same time, we can still be surprised at the religious interest present in the pluralistic, nominally Christian contemporary culture. The resilience of the religious spirit outside the institutional Church is significant. But nostalgic responses should not be misinterpreted as a serious commitment to God or the Christian community.

Are there not non-manipulative and open ways to awaken and develop the religious aspect of ourselves? Many other important aspects of our global experience are being explored through the media: our use of resources, and economic and cultural development, for example. Most of us are not research economists but we can follow and at times participate through the press and the electronic media in the public debates that surround these issues. We have become concerned about issues like war and peace and world hunger mainly through the media. It is a theatrical stage, a public forum. Perhaps the Christian community can also air some of its concerns there.

In one sense, medieval cathedrals were mass culture efforts. They brought diverse artistic talents into a unified public expression. What is missing today is a new religious language in our various arts, architecture and script-writing. A period in which language joins spirituality and the means of construction produces cathedrals or their modern equivalent. There is a décollage between our religious language, which is Victorian for the most part (that is, pastoral and romantic metaphor), and our spirituality, which lacks a language but is nonetheless present and vibrant. The gap is here but people are searching for the expression.

Notes

1.   A.P. Flannery, O.P., ed., *The Documents of Vatican II* (New York: Pillar Books, 1975).

2.   *Ibid.*, 903-1014.

3.   December 7, 1965.

4.   The World Council of Churches prepared a document on the same topic in 1968. Fourth Assembly, Uppsala, Sweden, 1968, *Uppsala Report: Appendix XI: The Church and the Media of Mass Communication* (Geneva: World Council of Churches, 1968).

5.   Martin Marty, "Prophecy, Criticism and Electronic Media," *Media Development*, 28, no. 4 (1981), 30–33. See also Malcolm Muggeridge, *Christ and the Media* (Sevenoaks, Kent: Hodder and Stoughton, 1977).

6.   Jacques Cousineau, S.J., *Eglise et Mass Media* (Montreal: Office des Communications Social), 1973.

7.   In his book *Communicazione. Communione e chiesa* (Rome 1973), Enrico Baragli fills more than a thousand pages with texts from 1500 on that would today be loosely considered on the subject of the instruments of social communications.

8.   *Conclusions des journees 1957 de l'O.C.I.C.* (La Havane), cited in Cousineau, 13. Translation my own.

9.   Quoted in W.M. Abbott, S.J., ed., *The Documents of Vatican II* (New York: Association Press, 1966), 703.

10.   Karlhein Schmidthüs, "Decree on the Instruments of Social Communication," in *Commentary on the Documents of Vatican II*, ed. H. Vorgrimler, trans. R. Strachan, vol. 1 (New York: Herder and Herder, 1967), 89–104.

11.   *Acta Synodalia Sacrosancti Concilii Vaticani II*, vol. 2, pt. 6 (Typis Polyglottis Vaticanis, 1974), 19, 36, 49. Votes on chapter 1: total 2168, affirmative 1832, negative 92, affirmative with reservation 243; chapter 2: total 2126, affirmative 1893, negative 103, affirmative with reservation 125.

12.   First ballot: present 2132, affirmative 1788, negative 331, spoilt 13; second ballot: present 2112, affirmative 1598, negative 503, spoilt 11.

13.   Avery Dulles, "The Symbolic Structure of Revelation," *Theological Studies*, 41, no. 1 (1980), 51–73; and Guy Lafon, "Communication and Revelation," *Lumen Vitae*, vol. 36, no. 3 (1981), 359–71.

14.   Avery Dulles, *The Church Is Communication*, MI Booklet no. 1 (Rome: Multimedia International 1972).

15.   Pontifical Commission for the Means of Social Communication, *Pastoral Instruction for the Application of the Decree of the Second Vatican Ecumenical Council on the Means of Social Communication* (*Communio et Progressio*) (Washington: United States Catholic Conference, 1971).

16.   A short general essay on *Communio et Progressio* can be found in J. Harrington, "Media of Social Communication and the Church," *New Catholic Encyclopedia*, vol. 17 (Washington, D.C.: McGraw-Hill, 1967), 400–03.

COMMENTARY ON THE

Decree on the Church's Missionary Activity

Ad Gentes

CARL STARKLOFF

Considering the epochal nature of Vatican II and the Church's years of struggle during that time to re-express its nature, it is not surprising that any statement about its missionary identity should undergo a painful emergence into the light. And so it was. The first draft of a document on missions proposed to the Council after it convened on October 11,1962, was the work of a preparatory commission that had laboured from April 17, 1961, until February 2, 1962. This commission had begun with twenty-two bishops from Eastern and Western Europe, North and Latin American, and Asia. It was later augmented with thirty-two more consultants, drawn heavily from religious orders, and over-weighted with members of European background.[1] The president of the Council's missionary commission was Cardinal Agaianian, assisted by twenty-four members (later increased to twenty-nine) drawn from among missionary bishops. This group was of a greater racial mix.

The initial draft was unpromising, adhering to a highly institutional format. It focussed on mission governance, clerical discipline, religious community life, norms for sacramental practice, "Christian discipline," clergy studies, and models of missionary co-operation based on a tight hierarchical structure. As was the case with *Lumen Gentium*, the first schema on the Church, to which the final mission decree is closely related, this document drew strong disapproval from the ranks of the bishops. A plenary meeting of the Council's missionary commission, from March 20–29, 1963, struggled tediously to produce a considerably more sophisticated statement. This document included a section on principles for mission and gave some attention to the role of the laity in mission work. But the debate was only beginning and a great tug-of-war developed among the Council Fathers.[2] By December 3, 1963, still another schema emerged with greater emphasis on theoretical development.

125

There followed much conciliar consultation between January and May 13, when the full commission approved a schema whose title had been changed from *De Missionibus* to *De Activitate Missionale*, indicating a stronger praxis orientation. The debate of November 1964 was marked by a historic appearance of Pope Paul VI in the Council hall. Nonetheless, in spite of this indication by the Holy Father of a sense of urgency about the debate, most missionary bishops rejected the schema. They had felt slighted and marginalized by its still shallow treatment of the subject. Even at this point, no concern was being shown for the questions of culture, local Churches, inter-religious dialogue, ecumenism, or other matters that would eventually come to characterize the tone of Vatican II. Although this schema was officially rejected, it was actually "better than its reputation," according to Brechter; by this time the *Dogmatic Constitution on the Church* had established the missionary nature of the Church as a whole.[3]

A new sub-commission began work on a revised schema on January 12, 1965, and produced a document for the conciliar plenary session of March 29–April 3. This new text was destined to become the official decree, with one major exception. Whereas the proposed schema sought to include the section on "particular Churches" as a mere article under chapter 2 on missionary work, the revised version gave the local Church question a chapter all its own. The final document was approved on October 15, 1965, and ruled in force on June 29, 1966.

HIGHLIGHTS OF THE DELIBERATIONS

We can enrich our understanding of the decree by examining the more critical points of argumentation in the conciliar debates and in the bishops' written opinions. At the outset of the final document there is the crucial doctrinal statement, "The Church on earth is by its very nature missionary" with its origin in the mission of the Son and Holy Spirit from the Father.[4] Brechter comments that this principle, based on the concept of the Church as universal sacrament of salvation and developed in the *Dogmatic Constitution on the Church*, grows out of the Church's renewed consciousness of its own nature.[5] Corollaries of this principle have only begun to be developed in subsequent missiology, although one finds many examples of creative thinking in the opinions of Bishop Richard Cleire on mutuality, for example. If the whole Church is to be missionary, world missions would emanate from Africa, Asia, and India, for example, after the European missionaries have done their work.[6] The Church never ceases to be missionary. When "young Churches" have become more established, they too can maintain life only by sending out emissaries—perhaps to the very parts of the world whence came the first missionaries to their land.

The trinitarian basis of mission is a second vital doctrinal principle: the Father, as fountain of love, sends forth the Son into the world to draw it into the community of divine life.[7] *Ad Gentes* gives striking recognition to the doctrine of the Holy Spirit sent by the Father to ensure that salvation would be proclaimed not only in Palestine but throughout the world. Important here is the recognition of the Spirit's work in the world even before Christ was glorified. Brechter writes, "The missionary would do well to observe carefully what the Holy Spirit has already affected among his hearers, so as to link up with it and build on it."[8]

The decree moves on to discuss the missionary Church as much. This Church is expected to walk the same road which Christ walked—poverty, obedience, service, self-sacrifice, as well as resurrection.[9] Missionary activity is a temporary Church vocation until the Gospel has been preached to all the nations before the Lord's return.[10]

A significant point for mission theology arises here. Brechter points out that, until this time, modern Roman Catholic mission theology had developed according to two schools of thought. One of those was the Christocentric and personal theology elaborated by Josef Schmidlin, who followed the thought of Gustav Warneck. In this, mission is the task of converting humanity through proclamation of the Gospel and summoning people to turn to Christ. The other school was that of Pierre Charles and Andre Seumois—the "Church-planting" theory that stresses the founding and building of indigenous Churches; this is comparable to the thought of Donald McGovran in Protestant circles.

Both of these schools emphasize institutions, and Brechter commends *Ad Gentes* for developing the "People of God" theology as found in *Lumen Gentium* into a more creative synthesis of mission ecclesiology.[11]

Articles 7 and 8 of *Ad Gentes* complete this section of doctrinal principles. First, mission activity is founded in the will of God, who calls all peoples to be his own people. Second, mission is "intimately bound up with human nature and its aspirations,"[12] and Christ ought not to be presented to such aspirations as a complete foreigner. The Gospel is not a force for cultural destruction, but one of transformation and fulfilment: "So whatever goodness is found in the minds and hearts of men, or in the particular customs and cultures of peoples, far from being lost, is purified, raised to a higher level and reaches its perfection..."[13] Brechter cites the *Retractationes* 1, 12, 3 of St. Augustine to show one source of the theory of fulfilment:

> The reality itself which is now called the Christian religion was also present among the ancients and was not lacking from the very beginning of the human race, until Christ appeared in the flesh. From then on, the true religion, which had always existed, began to be called the Christian religion.[14]

Ad Gentes is one of the many steps taken by Vatican II to let the world know that the Church does not consider it to be under divine condemnation but called to further transformation.

Chapter 2 of the decree deals with actual mission work. Article 1, on Christian witness, is noteworthy for its call to missionaries to be "familiar with their [all peoples'] national and religious traditions and uncover with gladness and respect those seeds of the Word which lie hidden among them."[15] The principles behind this exhortation were among the most hotly debated among the bishops. One school was represented by Cardinal Gracias of Bombay, who registered a deep suspicion of the notion of dialogue with non-Christian traditions: the Church's vocation rather is to bring the truth to those who do not possess it, and not to share with other religious on any basis of equality.[16] He attacked "progressive missiologists" here for failing to emphasize the Church as the divinely instituted means of salvation, which preaches the Cross as a sign of contradiction calling people to repent of their sins. It is interesting that Cardinal Gracias called for formation of clergy in "the primacy of love for acquiring wisdom," as opposed to scholastic learning. It is unclear whether the cardinal was advocating the effective development of clerics according to Gospel principles or attacking critical theological thought.[17] The opposing argument to Cardinal Gracias' is again represented by Bishop Cleire's emphasis on inter-cultural and ecumenical collaboration.[18]

"Particular Churches"—chapter 3 in the final draft—could well mark the decree as a missiological milestone. One must examine, however, the debates and opinions on chapter 2, "De Ipso Opere Missionali," in order to understand the struggle involved in its formation. It was originally divided into four sections: on gospel preambles, on preaching and assembling the People of God, on forming the Christian community, and on particular Churches. Brechter shows how the Council Fathers finally rejected the notion of *preambula fidei* thereby rendering questionable the value of much mission activity prior to actual preaching.[19] One sees here the discussions in theology before Vatican II, when the dominant position leaned towards a dominance of apologetics that would "prepare" people to see the "reasonableness" of the Gospel. Brechter credits the influence of Martin Buber with the establishment of an atmosphere more oriented towards dialogue rather than pre-evangelical polemics.[20]

The debates of the Council Fathers on dialogue with local traditions eventually promoted the section on particular Churches to the status of a full chapter. Once again, the arguments of Cardinal Gracias and Bishop Cleire typify the divergent views on "points of contact" between the Gospel and local cultures. Cardinal Gracias sought to emphasize that, without Christ, the other religions remain not only "imperfect," but "truncated" and "distorted."[21] Thus, he identified more with neo-orthodox Protestant "crisis theology" than with fulfilment theory. The focus of such theological method is on the Cross as a sign of divine judgment on all cultures and "religions." Cardinal Gracias, in fact, extended this confrontational theology into the Protestant camp as well, even denying to non-Roman Christians the right to propagate the Gospel.[22]

Other bishops and religious superiors, however, argued from the new paradigm set forth in the images of the texts of *Lumen Gentium* and *Gaudium et Spes*. Bishop Griffins, for example, argued that there should be mutual respect and "normal human relations" between cultures rather than attitudes of superiority.[23] Non-Roman Christians should not be objects of Roman Catholic preaching, wrote Bishops Geiger and Swamidoss Pillai.[24] Bishop Riobe insisted that at least a brief mention be made that non-Christian religions could be a preparation for the Gospel.[25]

In the debate over the Gospel-culture interaction, Bishop Cleire's carefully written opinion seems to have been significant; its tone can be seen in the final draft. He stated that *les espaces humains* of the great religions form a coherent and homogeneous world. Here that thinking of configurational and Gestalt psychology is influential in cultural matters: a culture is an integral whole whose unity must be respected by preachers of the Gospel.[26] To evangelize such worlds, the Church must have a view of the whole, and set its goals in harmony with human needs. Bishop Cleire connected this insight with the growth of "young" or recently founded Churches, involving profound adaptation of their liturgy, theology, law, religious life, and ecclesiology.[27] He wrote about the "assumption" of essential elements that characterize each large cultural area. New converts should be encouraged to follow a way of life in accord with their own customs, languages, and symbols, as they strive to live the Gospel. Respect must be maintained for the genius of a people, or the living spirit within its culture.[28] His argument manifests the spirit, if not the direct influence, not only of Pierre Charles, but also of Paul Tillich, whose "Gestalt of Grace" is symbolized in the delicately balanced tension between Gospel protest and cultural integrity.[29]

Considering the hectic process of its creation, the final document reads rather serenely on this point:

> This manner of acting will avoid every appearance of syncretism and false exclusiveness; the Christian life will be adapted to the mentality and character of each culture, and local traditions together with the special qualities of each national family, illumined by the light of the gospel, will be taken up into a Catholic unity.[30]

The remaining chapters of *Ad Gentes* are significant because they respond practically to the principles elaborated in the first three chapters. Chapter 4, "Missionaries," advocates a training that emphasizes both strong and special spiritual preparation as well as formation in cultural and linguistic studies.[31] Brechter relates this chapter to *Maximum Illud* of Benedict XV: the missionary's basic handbook is the Bible, carefully nuanced by studies in ethnology and the science of religions.[32] Bishop Cleire had registered a demand for a re-evaluation of the missionary vocation and the nurturing of it, relating this to the need to form a truly local clergy in the light of their own culture.[33]

Chapter 5, "The Organization of Missionary Activity," emphasizes the role of bishops, in accord with *Lumen Gentium*. As Brechter observes, however, the office of Propagation of the Faith (to be reorganized) emerges with renewed power and responsibility. Brechter also criticizes the Council for imposing so much work on a commission of twenty-four members scattered over the world, scheduled to meet only twice annually, in addition to the office of Propaganda Fide. Thus, the cardinals still remain the ultimate power,[34] in opposition to a strong call from many sources for local governance by stable ecclesial institutions adapted to local needs.[35] A footnote in the Abbott edition of Vatican II documents stresses that any reform of Propaganda Fide is to be in line with the Council's principle of collegiality.[36]

Chapter 6, "Co-operation," emphasizes the People of God as a sign to all nations. This theological principle is given institutional form. Bishops, while consecrated for one diocese, are called for the salvation of the whole world;[37] they therefore bear the task primarily of leading world evangelization. To assist them, the Council calls on diocesan clergy, religious communities, and those involved in the formation of priests to inculcate in their students a spirit of mission awareness. Article 41 is devoted to the vocation of the laity, especially those who are in a position to form missionaries through specialized training.[38] Brechter's comment here is significant not only for formation but for the future of the theological enterprise: "It is less a matter of lectures on missiology than of a close interweaving of fundamental ideas of the theology of mission throughout all the various branches of theology."[39]

EFFECTS IN THE CHURCH

In a short paper it is possible to discuss only some general consequences following on *Ad Gentes*. Since Vatican II, numerous commissions have been established in the Church throughout the world to implement the declarations on non-Christian religions and religious liberty, and the decrees of *Gaudium et Spes* and *Ad Gentes*. Roman commissions have worked to establish dialogue with other religions and cultures. This work is distinct from actual missionary proclamation, although the distinction has not yet been adequately clarified.

The discussions of the differences between evangelization, liberation, and development in the light of cross-cultural dialogue, has caused some anxiety.[40] In general, although much remains to be done, the decree on missionary activity, like the rest of the work of Vatican Council II, has ushered in a new epoch in mission work.

Theological reflection introduced by *Ad Gentes* and the general spirit and praxis enlivening its creation, points to the paradoxical tension and the intimate relationship between Christian faith and culture. One brief lecture by Karl Rahner has received considerable attention.[41] Rahner argues there that Vatican II ushered the Church into a "third epoch." The Church's original matrix was the Jewish cultural world, from which it quickly emigrated into the Hellenistic and thus the European world, and became a European Church. Now, says, Rahner, it is hearing the call to a new epoch, that of "the world Church."[42] The implications of this are many and critical. It is easy to empathize with the waves of culture shock spreading over a Church that is releasing its two millenia of European moorings.

But the Church can abide in the spirit of that first epochal change—recorded in Acts 15—only by carefully examining those religious and cultural norms that it may have held so long to be absolute. To cite Brechter's commentary once more: "It is a depressing historical fact that, except in Western Europe and in the New World, the Church has not been able to incorporate and transform any alien culture. It has not become entirely native anywhere, but has everywhere remained western."[43] But is even this claim verifiable? Has the Church in the Western Hemisphere indeed become indigenous, or has it simply become an "adjusted" European immigrant Church? These questions lead us to our concluding reflections.

THE EFFECTS ON THE CHURCH IN CANADA

One frequently hears the call for a "theology with a Canadian face"—a phrase that seems to have two different but related meanings. First, it may be a theology like those of such thinkers as John Courtney Murray and Harvey Cox, or the Black and the Social Gospel theologians and others in the United States. In the stricter sense of the word "mission" adopted by Vatican II, these are not missionary theologies. Yet, the work of these thinkers rarely mentioned the Amerindian people, those to whom the "New World" mission was directed—at least by the Roman Catholic Church. This omission indicates the deep problem of ethnocentrism in Euro-North American thinking. As yet, little has been done to build a theology of cultural pluralism in North America, even though countless Amerindian representatives have maintained that the root of their oppression is buried deep down in cultural imperialism.[44]

North Americans of European ancestry have, in fact, developed only a derivative of European culture with its languages and traditions, and instilled with a certain "New World" spirit. This process has indeed produced new approaches to a theology of religion and culture. Even for Euro-Americans, however, the greater challenge relates to a reconciliation with the people of this soil on which we live and, one might say, with the very soil itself. Indigenous peoples must therefore find and be encouraged in their own theological idiom, whether it be Christian or not. Of course, the critical reflection on religious experience is only a recent experience for Amerindian people, but theology is now being created by Natives, both to interpret their own traditional or Christian experience and to critique the Euro-American theory and practice.

"Particular Church" and "local Church" are phrases occurring frequently among Roman Catholic Natives. In many areas throughout Canada, most notable in the West, this theme means both an inculturation of the Gospel into Native forms and the beginning of a practice of the "Three-Self" principle of Church (self-government, self-support, self-propagation). East of Manitoba, the matter of inculturation is more complex. Because so many Natives have embraced a Christianity that called them away from tribal roots and symbolism over a longer period of time, the idea of inculturation seems strange to them, and perhaps even oppressive. Even in the East, however, Natives are becoming more concerned about their religious traditions and how they are to relate to them as Catholics. One major concern is the issue of Native clergy and leadership and how clerical celibacy and seminary training are obstacles to this.

The ongoing mission praxis in Canada would seem to require sensitive and long-term dialogue between theologians of the "mainstream" and Native representatives. It may be suggested that theology arising from such exchange should be written for now on loose-leaf pages rather than in printed books, to use an expression of Robert McAfee Brown in a somewhat different context.[45] Fundamentally, it must be Native people who build their own theology, but the centuries-long intermingling requires a collaborative effort in which all parties engage in "the self-corrective process of learning." The missionary Church will have to carry its role lightly, yet still be prepared to carry it, to facilitate the growing self-awareness of the Native Church.

In the fall of 1982, the Toronto School of Theology and the Ecumenical Forum of Canada collaborated on a two-day seminar on mission, focussing on Canadian aboriginal rights. The featured speaker was Peter Kelly, an Ojibway band chief from Kenora, Ontario. The audience, which had come to hear Mr. Kelly speak about Native rights, heard instead a life history and a narrative of the speaker's own dreams, with a short allusion at the end to the wild rice harvest controversy. It occurred to me that until our Church and our society can understand why this presentation took such a turn, empathetic dialogue will be impossible. The challenge to the Church in Canada—and in the world—would seem to be to learn how to undergo a "paradigm shift"[46] in thinking if it is to do mission in the pattern of Vatican II.

Notes

1. Heinrich Suso Brechter, "Decree on the Church's Missionary Activity," in *Commentary on the Documents of Vatican II*, ed. Herbert Vorgrimler, vol. 4 (Freiburg: Herder, 1969), 88.
2. *Ibid.*, 94.
3. *Ibid.*, 97.
4. A.P. Flannery, ed., *The Documents of Vatican II* (New York: Pillar Books, 1975). The Latin version reads: "Unde missiones, quae ex ipsa natura ecclesiae profluent, nihil aliud sunt quam aperatio qua ecclesia Corpus Christi visibiliter extendi. Quae ecclesia tota est missionaria...*Actus Synodalia Sacrosancti Concilii Oecumenici Vaticani II*, vol. 3, pars 6 (Roma: Typis Polyglottis Vaticanis, 1975), cited henceforth as *TPV III*. The Latin reads literally: "Wherefore, missions, which flow from the very nature of the Church, are nothing other than the operation by which the Church as the Body of Christ extends herself visibly."
5. Brechter, *Missionary Activity*, 113.
6. *TPV III*, 721.
7. *Ad Gentes*, nos. 2, 3.
8. Brechter, *Missionary Activity*, 115. See the excellent article by Orthodox Bishop Georges Khodr, "The Economy of the Holy Spirit," in *Mission Trends No. 5*, ed. G.H. Anderson and T.F. Stransky, C.S.P. (Grand Rapids Eerdmans, 1981), 36–49.
9. *Ad Gentes*, no. 5.
10. *Ibid.*, no. 9.
11. A more creative and less institutionalist interpretation might be given to Charles' theory in the light of his "forme de l'eglise" concept. See Pierre Charles, S.J., *Les dossiers de l'action missionaire* (Louvain: Editions de L'Aucam, 1938), 33, 45, 65.
12. *Ad Gentes*, no. 8.
13. *Ibid.*, no. 9.
14. Brechter, *Missionary Activity*, 123.
15. *Ad Gentes*, no. 11.
16. *TPV III*, 677.
17. *Ibid.*, 679.
18. *Ibid.*, 706.
19. Brechter, *Missionary Activity*, 126.
20. *Ibid.*, 127–28.
21. *TPV III*, 677.
22. *Ibid.*, 683.
23. *Ibid.*, 750.
24. *Ibid.*, 753, 841.
25. *Ibid.*, 819.
26. *Ibid.*, 706.
27. *Ibid.*, 711.
28. *Ibid.*, 718. For an excellent description of the "genius" idea, see Pietro Rossano, "Christ's Lordship and Religious Pluralism," in *Christ's Lordship and Religious Pluralism*, ed. G.H. Anderson and T.F. Stransky, C.S.P. (Maryknoll, N.Y.: Orbis Books, 1981).
29. Charles, *L'Action missionaire*. One might also see here the influence of Paul Tillich's "Gestalt of Grace" theory, which seeks a balanced tension between gospel witness and cultural integrity. See Paul Tillich, *The Protestant Era* (Chicago: University of Chicago Press, 1957), 206–21.

30. *Ad Gentes*, no. 22.

31. *Ibid.*, 843.

32. Brechter, *Missionary Activity*, 155–56.

33. *TPV III*, 725.

34. Brechter, *Missionary Activity*, 163–64.

35. *TPV III*, 726.

36. Walter M. Abbott, S.J., ed., *The Documents of Vatican II* (New York: Guild Press, 1966), 620f.

37. *Ad Gentes*, no. 38.

38. Brechter voices another concern on this point: "The task of the missions consists in gathering together the People of God, not in establishing a hierarchical clerical Church." *Missionary Activity*, 149.

39. *Ibid.*, 178.

40. For an excellent sampling of all these discussions, see the volumes of *Mission Trends*, ed. Anderson and Stransky.

41. See Karl Rahner, S.J., "Towards a Fundamental Theological Interpretation of Vatican II," *Theological Studies*, 40 (1979), 716–27.

42. In this connection, see *The Jurist* (Winter/Spring, 1979) for articles on the concept of *missio* in relation to ecclesiology, evangelization, worship, social justice, ministry, ministerial jurisdiction, and Church structure from a canonical viewpoint. *Missio* is here treated as the basic criterion for adaptation in the Church. In his article "The Established Church as Mission: The Relation of the Church to the Modern World," 4–39, R.D. Haight, S.J., studies the implications of the mission paradigm of Church, continuing his argument from "Mission: The Symbol for Understanding the Church Today," in *Why the Church*, ed. W.F. Burghardt, S.J., and W.D. Thompson, S.J. (New York: Paulist Press, 1977), 76–105.

43. Brechter, *Missionary Activity*, 150.

44. Vine Deloria, Jr., "A Native American Perspective on Liberation," in *Mission Trends No. 4*, ed. G.H. Anderson and T.F. Stransky, C.S.P. (Grand Rapids: Eerdmans, 1970), 261–270.

45. Robert McAfee Brown, "Liberation Theology: Paralyzing Threat or Creative Challenge?" in *Mission Trends No. 4*, 5.

46. For a creative explanation of "paradigm shift" in missiology, see Charles H. Kraft, *Christianity in Culture* (Maryknoll, N.Y.: Orbis, 1979), 5 *et passim*.

Declaration on the Relationship of the Church to Non-Christian Religions

Nostra Aetate

OVEY MOHAMMED

The *Declaration on the Relationship of the Church to Non-Christian Religions, Nostra Aetate* is only five pages in length. These five pages are made up of 178 lines, of which seventy-two deal with Judaism, nineteen with Islam, six with Hinduism, six with Buddhism, and four with all the other religions of the world. This proportion is puzzling when we call to mind that there are about fifteen million Jews in the world, that the religion of the Muslims, who number about eight hundred million, is the fastest growing religion today, and that the population of Asia, which numbers over two and one half billion, is predominantly Hindu and Buddhist.

Why is the treatment of the world religions so uneven? Perhaps the story behind the document may provide the answer.

This document arose from the desire of Pope John XXIII to have a declaration on the relation of the Church to the Jews. In keeping with this wish, on September 18, 1960, he commissioned Cardinal Bea's Secretariat for Promoting Christian Unity to draft such a declaration, although it was not, strictly speaking, a matter of Christian unity. Christian unity refers to relationships among Christians—Catholics, Protestants, and Eastern Orthodox; the ground of such unity is the shared Christology which is particular to Christendom.

The first draft of the declaration on the Jews was presented to the Council at its second session on November 18, 1963, as chapter 4 of the *Decree on Ecumenism, Unitatis Redintegratio*. It was brief and reasonably clear in its repudiation of anti-Semitism. It stated that the "Church of Christ recognizes that the beginnings of her faith and election are found in the Patriarchs and Prophets," that Catholics cannot forget that the Church "is the continuation of that people with whom God was pleased, in his mercy, to establish the Old Covenant," that it was "unjust to call them [the Jews] 'deicides' because it was the sin of all mankind that caused the suffering and death of Christ," and that the Church "deplores and condemns the persecutions of the Jews which have taken place in recent times."[1]

The declaration became the occasion of bitter disputes. Some conservatives objected to any mitigation of the collective guilt of the Jews for the Crucifixion. Some bishops from Islamic countries thought that the document might be interpreted as a political move by the Church to recognize the state of Israel. The Vatican Secretary of State argued that the declaration should be shortened and placed in the document on the Church to avoid possible reprisals from Muslim governments. Some Council Fathers, from the Near East in particular, insisted that the declaration include a reference to Islam; others went as far as to demand a declaration that expresses the attitude of the Church to all non-Christian religions.

Because of these disputes, a new statement was ordered, this time to be composed with the advice of the Co-ordinating Commission of the Council.

The second draft of the declaration on the Jews emerged in the third session of the Council on November 20, 1964. This was no longer a part of the *Decree on Ecumenism*, but became a part of the longer *Declaration on the Relationship of the Church to Non-Christian Religions*. Some still objected to what was said about the Jews, and the test had to be rewritten further to meet these objections. And then there was an additional problem. In his Passion Sunday homily of April 1965, Pope Paul VI spoke of the Jews in a way that was immediately interpreted as evidence of anti-Semitism in the Pope himself. Discussing the Gospel account of the Crucifixion, Pope Paul said that it is "a grave and sad page because it narrates the conflict, the clash between Jesus and the Jewish people, a people predestined to await the Messiah, but who, just at the right moment, not only did not recognize Him, but fought Him, strove against Him, and finally killed Him."[2]

After much wrangling, the revised draft that came to the floor at the fourth session of the Council was accepted and promulgated on October 28, 1965.

This final statement was, however, quite unsatisfactory from a Jewish point of view. It asserted that Christ, "who is our peace has through his cross reconciled Jews and Gentiles and made them one in himself." To many Jews, this seemed an involved way of saying that Judaism no longer had any real reason for existence. Moreover, although it issued no direct call for their conversion, the declaration noted that "the Church awaits the day, known to God alone, when all peoples will call on God with one voice" and serve him with one accord (4).

The final text of the declaration was also considerably weaker than the original draft. The earlier draft had said that the "Jewish people should never be presented as a people rejected of God or accursed or guilty of deicide." The final text stated that the "Jews should not be spoken of as rejected or accursed" by God. Although the word "deicide" was not used in the final text, when it came to the question of the guilt of the Jews for the Crucifixion, the text read: "Even though the Jewish authorities and those who followed their lead pressed for the death of Christ, neither all Jews indiscriminately at that time, nor Jews today, can be charged with the crimes committed during the passion." This is just another way of saying that Christ's suffering could be charged against some of the Jews.

Furthermore, the word "condemns" was excised from the phrase "deplores and condemns" of the original draft in describing the past persecutions of the Jews. The final text stated that the Church "deplores all hatreds, persecutions, displays of anti-Semitism levelled at any time or from any source against the Jews." If this statement had been made before Hitler, it probably would have been welcomed by nearly all Jews. As it stood, however, the excision was widely regarded as an inadequate compromise for a total condemnation and acknowledgment of the short-comings of the Church in confronting Nazi policies.

If the final text had been the original wording of the declaration, it may have been acceptable to the world's Jewish communities. But, the Vatican Council haggled over it for some four years. To many Jews, it appeared that the Jewish people were on trial during that time. As promulgated, the declaration was received by the Jews with public politeness, partly because they had the solid support for a stronger statement from the bishops of the United States and Canada, where there are more Jews than anywhere else in the world. Their chief regret was that the entire discussion about the declaration had revealed much prejudice against them in high places. It is impossible to avoid the conclusion that the Jews were let down.

It is clear that, because the *Declaration on the Relationship of the Church to Non-Christian Religions* grew out of the declaration on the Jews, the treatment of the other world religions passed almost unnoticed.

But it does not ignore them entirely. *Nostra Aetate* opens with a general observation on the unity of the human race—that men and women look to the various religions for answers to the profound mysteries of life. Hinduism, for example, not only contemplates the divine mystery and expresses it through an inexhaustible wealth of philosophical inquiry, but also responds to our existential situation through ascetical practices, deep meditation, and the trustful love of God.

137

Buddhism acknowledges the essential inadequacy of this changing world and teaches its followers how to attain a state of perfect liberation and supreme enlightenment in a devout and confident spirit. The other religions also propose ways, rules of life, and sacred rites to calm the hearts of men.

The declaration goes on to speak favourably about Islam. It states that the Church looks on Muslims with great esteem. It acknowledges that they worship the one God and praises their whole-hearted submission to him as well as their veneration of Jesus and Mary. In contrast to the comments of the Church in earlier centuries, this document points out that Muslims prize the moral life and honour God through prayer, fasting, and almsgiving. It admits to the hostility that prevailed between the two religions in former times and calls on Christians and Muslims to work for a better understanding of each other (3).

In addition, the declaration clearly states that non-Christians are by no means strangers to the divine truth, that the peoples of the world have always had a certain perception of that "hidden power" hovering over the events of human life, and that non-Christian religions "often reflect a ray of that truth which enlightens all men." The declaration therefore urges Christians to "acknowledge, preserve and encourage" through dialogue the "spiritual and moral truths" found among non-Christian religions (2).

The view that Christians may relate to non-Christians through dialogue presupposes a genuine respect on the part of Christians for non-Christians and their beliefs. The dialogue approach to non-Christians accords well with the entire tone of the Council; it marks a rather significant turning point in the history of the Church's relation with those outside its boundaries. It promises an end to any one-sided or impatient denigration.

A closer look at the declaration, however, reveals that it uses an underlying image of pilgrimage: human beings are on a pilgrimage toward union with God, a pilgrimage which God himself initiated. His offer of salvation was first made visible in the history of the people of Israel. It became fully and definitively manifest through the coming of Christ. It is Christ, present to all through the Church, who is the goal of the human quest for meaning and salvation.

In keeping with this image, the declaration ranks the various religions in relation to the Church. Thus, Judaism occupies a special place in the scheme of salvation because of its role in preparing the way for Christ and the Church. Islam, too, has a special relation to the Church because it shares in the same religious heritage. The other religions, notably Hinduism and Buddhism, are significant to the extent that they direct their followers to the true God and his offer of salvation, even though they do so obliquely. There exists, then, a hierarchy among the religions

of the world, a hierarchy with the Church at the top and the other religions related to it to the extent that they share in its understanding of
God's work in the world. Non-Christians in effect became unequal
partners in the dialogue.

The *Dogmatic Constitution on the Church, Lumen Gentium* repeats
the claim of the *Declaration on the Relationship of the Church to Non-
Christian Religions* that the Church is at the centre of the salvation of
the world. Again, it relates the non-Christian religions to itself concen-
trically. Moving out from the Church, the first circle takes in the Jews,
the second the Muslims, and the third those who seek the unknown God
in shadows and images, such as Hindus and Buddhists. The *Dogmatic
Constitution on the Church* then observes that, because all men and
women are ordained to the Church for their salvation, the Church must
preach its message to non-Christians to try to bring about their conversion to the Church (LG 16).

In other words, while the *Declaration on the Relationship of the
Church to Non-Christian Religions* and the *Dogmatic Constitution on
the Church* recognize that the non-Christian religions do indeed contain
elements of truth and goodness, and real moral and spiritual values,
these documents regard these religions as inferior to Christianity (NA 2;
LG 16; also AG 8, 9, 21).

In fact, both the *Dogmatic Constitution on the Church* and the *Decree
on the Church's Missionary Activity, Ad Gentes* see the good in them as
being only a "preparation for the Gospel" (LG 17; AG 3). The non-
Christian religions are good and worthwhile to the extent that they point
to God and invite people to share in the divine life; unless they are
connected in some way with the fullness of revelation that comes
through Christ and the Church, they cannot do so adequately. Moreover,
Ad Gentes notes that there is a tendency to pervert the truth because of
the effects of original sin (AG 9). The revelation of Christ must therefore purify and transform the truth and goodness of non-Christian
religions if they are to be truly worthwhile and valuable. This affirmation provides a motive for the Church to enter into dialogue with non-
Christians.

Elsewhere in this decree, Christians are told that they are to become
more aware of the truths and values present in non-Christian religions
through "patient and sincere" dialogue so that they may show that Christ
is the fulfilment of whatever is good and of value in these religions
(AG 11). Dialogue, then, is a first step in a gradual process of showing
non-Christians that Christ is "the way, the truth and the life"
(AG 8, 13).

Inspired by the Council, many Catholics have zealously pursued dialogue with non-Christians over the last twenty years, only to find the
tensions involved in the Church's understanding of dialogue. Many

non-Christians find the Church's interest in dialogue sudden, manipulative, and opportunist. They interpret the present interest of the Church in dialogue as a disguise for carrying on her missionary work, now that overt evangelization is impossible in many lands. They see the Church's interest in dialogue as a search for tolerance for itself, a tolerance which it has never extended to others. And they perceive the Church's understanding of dialogue as aimed not at an exchange of views but rather at the expansion of the influence of Catholicism.[3]

To complicate matters, because of the nature of Islam, Hinduism, and Buddhism, no organization has been or can be set up with the responsibility to take part in the dialogue on behalf of all Muslims, Hindus, and Buddhists respectively. Consequently, from their point of view, a religious dialogue can only take place between seekers and can have no official status. As well, among Hindus and Buddhists there is no such thing as orthodoxy. No wonder, then, that for these non-Christians a contradiction arises when Catholics speak of dialogue as part of the Church's mission. For them, this implies condescension and insincerity on the part of Christians; dialogue can never be a means, a bait, a ruse to convert anyone to the Church, not even in view of salvation. For them, dialogue is totally free from ulterior motives; it is a common search for truth, a march toward a common conversion, an enrichment that can never be adequately described from its starting point; dialogue can take place only where both parties are free to pursue the truth in utter sincerity and openness. Their experience of the last twenty years has shown that this is often not the case. They point out that Catholics entering into dialogue feel bound by the official teaching of the Church. They know that the fundamental liberty of Catholics with regard to the truth is curtailed by external authority. As a consequence, many non-Christians have given up on dialogue with Catholics, since Catholics are not prepared to publish, out of fear of the Church, what they say and admit to in dialogue.

In addition, there are the difficulties presented to Catholic theologians in the statement of the *Dogmatic Constitution on the Church* that God provides the means of salvation to those outside the Church because of his universal salvific will (LG 16). This brings up questions: If God's saving grace is present everywhere, and salvation is possible outside the Church, what is the nature of the Church and the sacraments? If all grace comes from Christ, and is available to all, even to those outside the Church, does it not follow that salvation does not depend unconditionally on the Church? If all grace comes from Christ, and is available to all, is there any point or urgency in preaching the Gospel? Are the non-Christian religions substantial means of salvation? What is the ultimate nature of the revelation of Christ?

The *Dogmatic Constitution on the Church* does not elaborate on these questions, and many others. Theologians are hard put to find satisfactory answers to them.

One cannot help but feel that *Nostra Aetate* is an attempt to correct some of the wrongs of the past rather than a fully conscious step into the furture. Since Trent, the Church has always taught that there is salvation outside the visible Church, while maintaining that the visible Church is necessary for salvation. Vatican II has restated this position. Although the declaration on the Jews admits that Judaism is the mother religion of Christianity, it treats the Jews in a statement along with Muslims, Hindus and Buddhists. And corrected though the Church's attitude to the Jews must be, this issue is in many ways a Western and Near Eastern one; the majority of the religiously committed people of the world do not live from the Judeo-Christian tradition.

Furthermore, the overtures to Hindus, Buddhists, and Muslims in the declaration are weak. In choosing to accentuate what these religions have in common with the Christian faith, *Nostra Aetate* has failed to come to grips with essential questions raised by these religions: What did God do through the Vedas, the scripture of Hinduism? What took place when Buddha received enlightenment? Is Muhammed a true prophet of God? A hierarchy of religions does not answer such questions and is also offensive to non-Christians. Therefore, when the declaration makes polite remarks about them, it succeeds only in being impolite. As Moffitt has observed, "These men of whom the Declaration speaks all happen to believe sincerely that their own religions are the truth. Yet they are addressed by the Council Fathers as if they were misguided children who surprisingly manifest on occasion a certain amount of good sense. The over-all impression created by the Declaration is certainly, though not intentionally, one of benign condescension."[4] Indeed, one cannot help but feel that the declaration is an attempt to put right some of the wrongs of the past rather than to take a fully conscious step into the future. Such a view should surprise no one, given the accidental circumstances under which it came into existence.

The heart of the problem in the document is the Church's theology of religions. Because of this, a theological explanation of dialogue and the encounter of religions was not provided. Perhaps a satisfactory solution to the problem would come when a theology of religions is sensitive to the stubborn fact of religious pluralism. Such a theology would attempt to be intellectually respectable, theologically convincing, spiritually satisfying, and emotionally acceptable to all partners in dialogue.[5]

Notes

1.   For a more comprehensive discussion of the many drafts of the declaration on the Jews and the Jewish reaction to them, see Paul Blanchard, *Paul Blanchard on Vatican II* (Boston: Beacon Press, 1966), 123–46.

2.   For an English translation of the homily, see the *National Catholic Reporter*, Apr. 14, 1965.

3.   See, for example, E. Berkovits, "Judaism in the Post-Christian Era," in *Disputation and Dialogue: Readings in the Jewish-Christian Encounter* , ed. Frank E. Talmage (New York: Ktav, 1975), 284–95; "Buddhist-Christian Encounter," *Pro Mundi Vita Bulletin*, 67 (July-Aug. 1967); "The Christian-Muslim Dialogue of the Last Ten Years," *Pro Mundi Vita Bulletin*, 78 (Sept.-Oct. 1978); "Hindu-Christian Dialogue in India," *Pro Mundi Via Bulletin*, 88 (Jan. 1982).

4.   John Moffitt, "Christianity Confronts Hinduism," *Theological Studies*, 30 (1969), 208.

5.   For an attempt to construct such a theology, see my "Christianity in a Religiously Plural World," in *Tradition and Innovation*, ed. J. B. Gavin (Regina: Campion College Press, 1983), 235–50.

COMMENTARY ON THE

Declaration on Religious Freedom

Dignitatis Humanae

COLIN CAMPBELL

Some very interesting questions emerge from a rereading of the Vatican II document The *Declaration on Religious Freedom, Dignitatis Humanae*, now that it has been with us in its final form for twenty years. How does the document strike us in an era that is both more sophisticated politically and less likely to have *deus ex machina* views of what Church documents can accomplish? What effects has the decree had on Church life? Did it advance the cause of religious freedom throughout the world? As Canadians, is there anything in particular that we can derive from the document?

WHAT WAS SAID

The various drafts of the document aroused very serious concerns among those who stood to lose ground in a liberalized view of the place of the Church in society. It threatened the oligarchical status of the Church in relation to other confessional groups within some states. By extension, it questioned the hegemony of hierarchies in some national Churches. For example, if religious tolerance suggests that the state can no longer ban artificial contraceptives, it becomes increasingly difficult to convince the Catholic laity that they do not have the right of conscientious judgment in this moral area. John Courtney Murray spoke to this point in a brief comment on the document:

> The declaration deals only with the minor issue of relgious freedom in the technical secular sense, it does not affirm a principle of wider import —that the dignity of man consists in his responsible use of freedom. Some of the conciliar Fathers...perceived that a certain indivisibility attaches to the notion of freedom...The text itself was flung into a pool whose shores are as wide as the universal Church. The ripples will run far.[1]

The document is confusing at the outset. On the one hand, it urges people to act upon their own judgment rather than from coercion.[2] But, it seems to add a rationalistic note by saying that responsible freedom will take root in "a sense of duty." While the document espouses a wide frame for religious freedom, such glosses stack the deck on the side of deference to Church authority:

> Religious freedom, in turn, which men demand as necessary to fulfill their duty to worship God, has to do with immunity from coercion in civil society. Therefore, it leaves untouched traditional Catholic doctrine on the moral duty of men and societies toward the true religion and toward the Church of Christ.[3]

In chapter 1, the document advocates the entrenchment of religious freedom in national constitutions.[4] The recognition of this principle must go beyond freedom of religious observance. It applies as well to the pursuit of religious truth. Once again, however, the state must impart this right on the grounds that it permits citizens to fulfil their "duty" to seek religious truth. Within these bounds, the document makes its clearest statement on behalf of open dialogue among believers:

> Truth, however, is to be sought after in a manner proper to the dignity of the human person and his social nature. The inquiry is to be free, carried on with the aid of teaching or instruction, communication, and dialogue. ... Moreover, as the truth is discovered, it is by a personal assent that men are to adhere to it.[5]

The document's explanation of open dialogue focusses almost exclusively on the obligations of the state. That is, it does not explain how the Church furthers free discussion of religious truth. For instance, a discussion of individual conscience stresses the "exercise of religion." Likewise, formal religious bodies must operate unemcumbered by the state.[6] Interestingly, the document here criticizes overzealous proselytism by noting that religious groups do not have licence to use coercive means or unseemly persuasion in winning converts; this sounds like a protest against evangelicals. A word is then inserted supporting freedom of choice between public and religious school systems.[7] The document, however, remains silent on such issues as exclusion of prayer from public schools—an act which can be interpreted as the displacement of religion from North American culture.

Chapter 2 examines in detail the role of freedom of religious conscience in relation to revelation. The text states emphatically that individuals should embrace the Christian faith freely, engaging as fully as possible their judgment.[8] It cites several Scriptural references indicating the respect for individual conscience that Jesus and the apostles used in their ministry. Beginning with section 13, the chapter also defines the parameters of the Church's rights in relation to society and individuals. The assertion that the Church shoulders pre-eminent responsibility for the salvation of all persons is the lynchpin of this treatment. We find here a restatement of many of the positions in chapter 1 about individual Christians' and the Church's civil liberties. As well, faithful who do not "attend to the sacred and certain doctrine of the Church" or disciples who do not strive to grasp the truth "ever more adequately" and proclaim it receive, at the least, oblique admonitions.[9]

THE EFFECTS OF THE DOCUMENT

It is difficult to establish—at least in rigorously analytic terms—exactly what effect the document has had. About religious freedom in the world, however, three principal areas of potential development suggest themselves: recognition of religious freedom in Communist countries, the issue of liberation theology in the Third World and the progress of ecumenism in advanced pluralistic societies.

Apart from the Solidarity movement in Poland, religious freedom has not gained much ground in Communist countries. Indeed, it would have been naive to expect that a document would either incite believers to demand greater religious freedom or stir regimes to greater acknowledgment of related civil liberties. However, Vatican II might claim a more general lasting effect on conditions in the Soviet Bloc. For instance, the introduction of the vernacular to ethnic and linguistic national groups in the Church can quicken national assertiveness. Poland provided the very favourable circumstances for such an effect. In fact, some observers debate whether sustained church attendance there reflects religiousness or nationalism.

More than any other development, the identification of some elements of national hierarchies and clergy with human rights and socioeconomic development has given the post-Vatican II era a place in the history books. Most of the contribution came through the auspices of The *Pastoral Constitution on the Church in the Modern World, Gaudium et Spes*. Those movements seeking human progress that base their appeals on Christian ideals raise their cause to the level of beliefs. No matter how much the traditionalists assert that the Church should stay out of politics and the market place, the right to proclaim the Social Gospel fits entirely within the frame of religious freedom. By the same token, the possibility of a dialogue on issues of liberation is most certainly essential to freedom of conscience among believers in the Church.

As with liberation, the ecumenical dimensions of the post-Vatican II era have taken root in other documents of the Council than simply

Dignitatis Humanae. If anything, this document would discourage other Christians, believers in non-Christian traditions and non-believers. For other Christians, it still speaks very much as the one, true Church—albeit a more conciliatory one; for non-Christian believers, it offers no explicit recognition; for non-believers, it scolds on the normal fare of church-state issues. Obviously, in the last twenty years relations between the Church and all three groups have improved greatly. However, the document has little that invites others to open discussions with our lot.

As noted above, the document uses different models for dialogue in society generally and the Church. This tactic does not advance very well the cause of individual conscience in the Church. With respect to society, the document condones the tenets of tolerance found in advanced pluralistic democracies more than any previous Church documents. Of course, a reasonably open discussion of the fundamental principles that govern society is what separates open from closed political systems.[10] In fact, pluralistic societies maintain much of their appeal by assuring their citizens that special claims will be accommodated eventually. Traditional hierarchical societies work only if individuals see themselves as subjects who must defer to the judgment of their leaders.[11]

While acknowledging the value of pluralism in society generally, the document's emphasis on authority in the Church makes it clear that different rules govern believers. Even twenty years after Vatican II, the hierarchy still demands essentially the same assent to its teachings as it did before. Closed systems tolerate some dissent by certain members because of their standing in and outside an institution. And, many members of the rank and file protest silently by disobeying those rules that cannot be monitored closely. Without putting too fine a point on it, these dynamics seem to characterize what has happened in the Church in response to the 1968 encyclical on birth control.

Within the Church, at least four strata coexist more or less amicably —the hierarchy, the operational officials (priests), the highly attentive membership (the educated and articulate laity and nonordained religious) and the rank-and-file believers. Of these groups, the first and third have developed the most in the post-Vatican II era. Bishops in most countries confer with one another much more now and have, as the American pastoral on war and peace indicates, addressed very creatively matters that cut to the very heart of believers' relations with the state. The attentives have worked effectively, largely through ginger groups, to pose issues to the hierarchy that would have rarely been raised before Vatican II. On the other hand, priests, after a spurt of activity in the late 1960's, have largely receded to the role of functionaries. Even the Jesuits have agreed to a modus vivendi with the Vatican whereby their theologians confine discussion of controversial issues to scholarly publications. As for the rank-and-file, parish councils, prayers and study groups, and small worship communities have not fulfilled the immediate post-Vatican II visions of a more participatory Church.

Recently in the United States, certain bishops made public statements that suggest a return among some in the hierarchy to tenets about the proper place of the clergy and the laity which hark to highly traditional, pre-Vatican II times. For instance, John J. O'Connor, the Archbishop of New York, appears firmly ensconced in a strongly hierarchical approach to Church authority. In a letter to his priests while Bishop of Scranton, he styled as "grave" such diverse issues as abortion, salaries for lay faculty in parochial schools and "misinterpretation and misuse" of the pastoral on war and peace. Leaders in subject-oriented societies characteristically couch their appeals in alarmist terms even when—as is the case with salaries and interpretation or use of a document—one would be hard pressed to justify such approaches. As well, Bishop O'Connor appeared to view his priests as ciphers:

> The pulpit is not the place for theological speculation. Our people are crying for fundamentals. They hear too many uncertain trumpets, are misled by too many Pied Pipers. When they come to Mass they deserve the teaching of Jesus as articulated for us by the Church, the councils, the magisterium, the Holy Father.[12]

As for ecumenism, he believed that it was a matter for the hierarchy:

> I intend to have a few quiet dinners to provide opportunities for quiet, friendly discussions with representatives of other church bodies. In some particularly sensitive areas, publicity can be more harmful than helpful.[13]

Events during the summer of 1984 provide us with even clearer evidence of a broadly based trend among bishops to question the implications of pluralistic tolerance on some key teachings. Specifically, some now impose standards for judging the public stances of contemporary Catholic politicians that they had set aside—or, at least, failed to invoke —for almost twenty years. In 1960, John F. Kennedy put to rest fears that his Catholicism might interfere with his upholding the Constitution:

> I believe in an America where the separation of Church and State is absolute—where no Catholic prelate would tell the President...how to act...where no public official either requests or accepts instructions on public policy from the pope, the National Council of Churches, or any other ecclesiastical source.[14]

The bishops of his day did not vigorously contest Kennedy's formulation. A concerted protest, however, arose from the hierarchy during the summer of 1984 when Mario Cuomo, Governor of New York, and Geraldine Ferraro, Democratic vice-presidential candidate, asserted that—while personally opposed to abortion—they do not believe they can seek to impose their views on the public. That is, they do not believe that they can press for such legislative actions as a constitutional amendment prohibiting abortion or exclusion of poor women seeking abortions from assistance through Medicaid.

The bishops' response to Ferraro simply marked the apogee of gradual movement from the Kennedy formulation and, more generally, from pluralistic tolerance. In isolated incidents, local ordinaries had spoken publicly against individual candidates and officeholders who refused to take a strong stance against abortion either in speeches or votes. Yet, concern over Governor Cuomo's and Representative Ferraro's abortion positions tipped the bishops toward a collective response. At the outset, this came in a statement by Bishop James W. Malone, president of the National Conference of Catholic Bishops, which questioned in general terms the validity of candidates' and office-holders' espousing a dichotomy between personal morality and public policy in certain issues.

Bishop Malone's document bears close inspection if for no other reason than it reflects how he and many of his colleagues have retreated to the traditional ground of hierarchical leadership. For instance, the statement styles bishops as teachers. At first blush, the reader might expect an elaboration of the role of teachers that acknowledges how clerics, religious leaders among the laity, scholars and parents take part—according to their station and talents—in this vital function for the Church. Instead, the statement, by a highly eliptical citing of a passage from the Vatican II document *Gaudium et Spes*, appears to appropriate for the hierarchy the entire teaching function:

> By preaching the truth of the Gospel and shedding light on all areas of human activity through her teaching and the example of the faithful, the Church shows respect for the political freedom and responsibility of citizens to foster these values [unacknowledged elipsis]. She also had the right to pass moral judgment even on matters touching the political order, whenever basic personal rights or the salvation of souls makes such judgments necessary.[15]

This quotation excludes two entire paragraphs, one that makes it clear the teaching function is shared by the successors to the apostles *and* those who assist them. The first of the omitted paragraphs also urges that "those who dedicate themselves to the ministry of God's Word use means and help proper to the gospel."[16] Donald Campion, the commentator for the Guild Press edition of the document, views this passage as an admission that some Church teaching authorities in the past have failed to give due regard to individual conscience and the proper distinctiveness of the religious and political domains.[17] Similarly, the second omitted paragraph registers the aspiration that the Church will not "lodge her hope in privileges conferred by civil authority" and even "renounce the exercise of certain acquired rights if it becomes clear that their use raises doubt about the sincerity of her witness."

Bishop Malone's statement recognizes that, among Catholics and others with similar moral convictions, legitimate disagreements do arise "over how moral principles should be applied to the current facts in the public policy debate."[18] But the document identifies abortion and direct military attacks on noncombatants as areas where there can be no disagreement. That is, hierarchical admonitions against such actions are "a direct affirmation of the constant moral teaching of the Catholic Church, enunciated repeatedly over the centuries, as in our day, by the highest teaching authority of the Church." Thus, the statement concludes, candidates do not satisfy "the requirements of rational analysis" in these cases by making their personal beliefs clear yet failing to "take practical steps to translate these into policies and practical programs."

The embargo on disagreement over abortion and direct attacks on noncombatants in war proves, in fact, to be at odds with a parallel treatment in the pastoral letter on war and peace. After making a convincing case that virtually every conceivable use of nuclear weapons would result in unacceptable numbers of dead among noncombatants, the pastoral pulls abruptly short by not condemning deterrence outright. It makes the case that such a position would require "highly technical judgments about hypothetical events."[19] The bishops' pursuit of this line of argument later in the document gives a very wide berth indeed to mitigating technical considerations:

> The church's teaching authority does not carry the same force where it deals with technical solutions involving particular means as it does when it speaks of principles or ends. People may agree in abhorring an injustice, for instance, yet sincerely disagree as to what practical approach will achieve justice.[20]

Later, in a brief word about the obligations of public officeholders toward avoiding war, the pastoral urges upon citizens respect for "the vocation of public service." Further, the bishops seemingly agreed on a minimalist example when suggesting how public officeholders could work toward world peace:

> One specific initiative which might be taken now would be the establishment of a task force including the public sector, industry, labor, economists and scientists with the mandate to consider the problems and

challenges posed by nuclear disarmament to our economic well-being and industrial output.[21]

Besides appearing to dampen the spirit of Vatican II and that of the pastoral on war and peace, Bishop Malone's statement, by stressing the abortion issue, seems to have legitimized pointed criticisms of Ferraro by individual bishops during the 1984 presidential campaign. For instance, Archbishop O'Connor stated on two occasions during the same weekend—one before news cameras while still in vestments—that she had inaccurately given the impression that the Church's teaching on abortion was not "monolithic."[22] When pressed to back this accusation, he later produced a copy of a letter that Ferraro and two other colleagues had sent to Catholic members of Congress. It notes the simple fact that various Catholics take different stances on abortion;[23] it says nothing about the formal teachings of the Church on the issue. Pursuing a similar line to his predecessor Archbishop O'Connor, Bishop James C. Timlin of Scranton—in a press conference during a visit by Ferraro to his diocese—characterized her stance on abortion as "absurd" and "not a rational position."[24] He added that in order to verify that she was a good Catholic, she "would have to say she is personally against abortion and will do all that she can, within the law, to stop the slaughter of innocent human beings." Later, Archbishop Bernard F. Law joined the debate with criticism of Ferraro based on an exclusive association of the Church's teaching authority with the hierarchy:

> The issue is, is this or is this not the church's position, and I think the persons who have the right to articulate the church's position are the bishops in union with the Bishop of Rome and that position is unambiguous, consistent and monolithic, with anyone speaking to the contrary notwithstanding.[25]

Formulations of the relationship between personal religious convictions and public policy initiatives such as Ferraro's might well strike the reader as far too facile. Even with the constraints of the American Consitution and the limits of the possible in a pluralistic system, Catholic political leaders—Ferraro included—have shown a decided lack of imagination in establishing the most favourable constitutional and legal structure politically feasible for the unborn. However, the bishops' interventions in 1984 seemed to have exceeded the bounds of respect for individual conscience and the spirit of open discourse put forward in *Dignitatis Humanae* and reaffirmed in the U.S. as recently as 1983 in the pastoral on war and peace.

The bishops cited above now claim a paramountcy in two issues —abortion and attacks on noncombatants—where dissent within the

Church will not be allowed. However, individual bishops have invoked this authority in specific cases only against Catholic politicians who do not believe they can support measures to restrict abortion. Thus, a justice issue arises. Whereas politicians supporting nuclear deterrence still enjoy sanctuary from personal and public criticism, those who fail to advocate anti-abortion legislation now open themselves to sanctions in the form of overt and personal criticism by the hierarchy.

CONCLUSION

What is the significance of *Dignitatis Humanae* for Canadians? Most readers would suppose that the document's words on the necessity of entrenched religious liberties were directed to nations with suspended constitutions or fundamental laws that do not explicitly provide religious freedom. Of course, neither Canada nor the United Kingdom had written consititutions at the time of the document's issue. Canada has since remedied this lapse. However, the Canadian and British cases point up a flaw in the conceptualization of the document. It did not seem to occur to the framers that nations can have religious freedom on the basis of convention rather than a written constitution. That the American bishops had the strongest hand in fashioning the document's thrust reveals itself in a bias toward formal constitutional provisions.

On various levels, the Canadian hierarchy seems to follow the spirit of the document more than its American counterpart. For a number of reasons, the Christian Churches in Canada had worked more ecumenically than their opposite numbers in the U.S., even before Vatican II. The United Church of Canada—an amalgam of Methodists and Presbyterians—set the stage early on for putting aside doctrinal, ethnic and regional divisions in the name of Church unity. As well, the Social Gospel has had a much stronger effect in Canada than in the U.S.[26] Although at first hesitant, members of the Catholic hierarchy have joined with senior churchmen of all faiths in working together on the moral implications of political, economic and social ills. The Council documents have played a significant role in all of this. One may still find pockets of bigotry here and there, but much interaction has taken place between the Churches, among both clerical and lay leaders.

Since Vatican II, the bishops have done an exceedingly good job in their collegial and consensual discernment of how various teachings should apply in Canada. To be sure, their work has been made easier because there are fewer of them than in the U.S. hierarchy. Nevertheless, they deserve much praise for the seriousness with which they engage in the collective dynamics. They have thus provided excellent witness to non-Catholics.

This favourable assessment does not appear to carry over to greater participation of the rank-and-file laity in the Church. The great influx of Catholic immigrants since World War II has changed the balance of ethnic groups in the Church, especially in English-speaking Canada. In that case, it will take some time for more participatory dynamics to begin, if they are even possible. In Quebec, the Church experienced a serious decline in observance through the sixties and seventies. Recent indications suggest a recovery. Although they are not flocking to church, young Quebeckers who practise their faith clearly expect to be able to participate.

In comparison to distinct separation of church and state in the U.S., in Canada the line between the two sectors is drawn much less sharply. For instance, the long-standing Canadian practice whereby provincial governments fund sectarian schools would be anathema to many Americans.

Since Vatican II, the hierarchy has been restrained in its direct arrangements between and comments upon political leaders, in part because of the Quiet Revolution and the accompanying decline of Catholicism in Quebec.[27] This does not suggest that Canadian bishops eschew controversial stances. It is significant that the bishops apparently continue to stand by their Social Affairs Commission 1982 report, namely "Ethical Reflections on the Economic Crisis," even though it drew a barrage of criticism. How else can we interpret the frequent recurrence of the document's themes in Pope John Paul II's speeches during his 1984 tour of Canada? However, the bishops have remained loath to style specific political initiatives as essential or to publicly criticize individual political leaders.

On the issue of abortion, for instance, Emmett Cardinal Carter protested privately to Prime Minister Pierre Trudeau over the failure of the Liberal government to provide protections for the unborn in the Constitution Bill ultimately passed in 1982. Trudeau assuaged Cardinal Carter's concerns by giving his personal assurances that the absence of a right to life provision in no way suggested that the government planned to liberalize existing legislation about abortion. Obviously, the 246 to 24 vote in favour of the Constitution Act included many Catholic members of Parliament. Only one cited the absence of a right to life provision as the reason behind his negative vote. A Roman Catholic priest serving as a New Democratic Party member abstained for the same reason. Determining the ultimate shape of the Constitution Act had presented Catholic MP's with a much clearer opportunity to ban abortions than is likely ever to present itself to American legislators. The Canadians chose to maintain a status quo which is moderately restrictive. That the Canadian bishops hardly protested at all suggests a regard for the limits of the art of the politically possible in pluralistic systems.

Notes

1.   John Courtney Murray, S.J., "Religious Freedom," in *The Documents of Vatican II*, ed. Walter M. Abbott, S.J. (New York: Association Press, 1966), 672–74.
2.   *Dignitatis Humanae*, in *The Documents of Vatican II*, ed. A.P. Flannery, O.P. (New York: Pillar Books, 1975), no. 1.
3.   Murray, "Religious Freedom," 677.
4.   *Ibid.*, 679.
5.   *Ibid.*, 680.
6.   *Ibid.*, 682.
7.   *Ibid.*, 683.
8.   *Ibid.*, 690.
9.   *Ibid.*, 694–95.
10.   Robert A. Dahl, *Polyarchy: Participation and Opposition* (New Haven: Yale University Press, 1971), 6–7.
11.   Gabriel A. Almond and G. Bingham Powell, Jr., *Comparative Politics: A. Developmental Approach* (Boston: Little, Brown, 1966), 59–60.
12.   Excerpts from a letter by Bishop John J. O'Connor of Scranton, Pennsylvania, to priests of his diocese (Aug. 1983), *New York Times*, Feb. 6, 1964.
13.   *Ibid.*
14.   Speech by John F. Kennedy to the Greater Houston (Texas) Ministerial Association, Sept. 12, 1960.
15.   *Gaudium et Spes*, no. 76.
16.   *Ibid.*
17.   Donald R. Campion, S.J., "The Church Today," in *The Documents of Vatican II*, ed. Walter M. Abbott, S.J. (New York: Association Press, 1966), 144.
18.   Text of statement by Bishop James W. Malone, president of the National Conference of Catholic Bishops (Aug. 9, 1984), *New York Times*, Aug. 10, 1984.
19.   National Conference of Catholic Bishops, "The Challenge of Peace: God's Promise and Our Response," *Origins*, 13, no. 1 (May 19, 1983), 1–32.
20.   *Ibid.*
21.   *Ibid.*
22.   Excerpts from remarks by Archbishop John J. O'Connor of New York at a press conference in Altoona, Pennsylvania (Sept. 8, 1984), *New York Times*, Sept. 10, 1984.
23.   Text of a cover letter dated September 20, 1982, by Congresspersons Geraldine A. Ferraro, Leon E. Panetta, and Thomas A. Daschle, *New York Times*, Sept. 11, 1984.
24.   "Ferraro Defends Her Abortion Stand, But Is Criticized by Scranton Bishop," *Washington Post*, Sept. 13, 1984.
25.   From an interview on Sept. 20, 1984, with Archbishop Bernard F. Law, *New York Times*, Sept. 23, 1984.
26.   Gregory Baum, *Catholics and Canadian Socialism: Political Thought in the Thirties and Forties* (Toronto: Lorimer, 1980), especially chap. 5.
27.   Kenneth McRoberts and Dale Posgate, *Quebec: Social Change and Political Crisis* (Toronto: McClelland and Stewart, 1980), 57–9.